THE LOST ART
OF GENERAL MANAGEMENT

ROB WAITE

Library of Congress Cataloging-in-Publication Data

ISBN: 0-9753030-090000

Cover design: Faye Klein

Printed in the United States of America.

Contents

This book is dedicated to my mother and father, and to my wife and three daughters.

My mother gave me her love of art, reading and writing. My father taught me pragmatism, financial conservatism and work/life balance. No better life education could I have received than the teachings of my loving parents.

To Karen, Laura, Sarah and Samantha, thank you for the support, encouragement and time I needed to write this book. I count my blessings every day because you are in my life.

Also, a note of thanks to Bill Drellow; a better editor no one could have. Without your dedication to the cause and your talent, this book would have been nothing more than an idea I once had.

Introduction

General management is a lost art. The ability to take a balanced perspective on business has been overlooked, maligned and bred out of the species *manageris modernus.*

As corporations have expanded and their functional silos have grown taller, managers have become functionally myopic in running the day-to-day operations of their individual areas. Moreover, since the compensation systems in place at most modern companies are built on achieving very specific localized goals, there's little reward today for time spent looking over the fence to widen one's perspective on how the business operates and makes its money. As a result, the average manager's ability to help the company achieve its financial objectives is seriously limited.

The loss of general management skills is not just an issue for large corporations. In many smaller businesses, entrepreneurs who are masters at managing their particular product or service have ignored the business side of their business (assuming they understood it to begin with). This accounts for the failure of many promising start-up enterprises.

The situation isn't helped by the fact that many of America's business schools emphasize theoretical management techniques and strategies while ignoring the more pragmatic, hands-on fundamentals of business. Because many freshly minted MBAs don't understand the core purpose of a business or how to manage one holistically, they face a difficult learning curve after landing their first major job.

My business career has been devoted to broadening my experience and perspective. I have lived and worked on three continents – North and South America and Europe. I've experienced and dealt with businesses in circumstances ranging from rapid growth start-ups to mature companies in crisis. My international experience also has given me the opportunity to operate in economic conditions ranging from currency crisis to hyperinflation, and from rapid expansion to pure depression.

The breadth of my experience has allowed me to work with hundreds of businesses and, therefore, hundreds of business models, strategies and plans. The common denominator at all of the successful businesses I've worked with, whether they were Global 100 companies or a building materials distributor in South America, was a core group of leaders who thought and acted as general managers – regardless of their title or functional accountabilities.

I've enjoyed the best possible business education – one based on real-life case studies that I could apply to my work. It enabled me to become a senior executive at three large, publicly traded companies before I was 40.

I'm just an average guy who grew up in Philadelphia, went to public schools and attended a state college. But I was lucky enough to have come across a number of very good general managers who mentored me. I can only claim to have had the good sense to listen to and learn from them.

I wrote this book to mentor others in the same way. My mission is to pass along the knowledge that will separate the reader from colleagues who may be functional experts but totally deficient in the broader skills of general management.

My premise is that managers who take the time to understand both the big picture and the pragmatic details of their individual functions not only are better able to manage their own functions, but also are seen as providing significantly greater value to their employers. Needless to say, this is the key to career advancement. In other words, an effective general manager has the ability to see a business both from 40,000 feet and right up close. More importantly, he or she knows when to remain at 40,000 feet and when to get down for a closer look.

While the art of general management has been lost, it can be rediscovered, relearned and re-deployed into American business. Mastering the art of general management is the measure of a manager's maturity and, most importantly, the measure of a manager's value to his or her business.

I refer to business as an art to further make the point that management is not an exact science. Many companies have spent millions on consultants in hopes of reducing the practice of management to a totally predictable plan. They fail to grasp two important things: First, business is just too messy for this. Human nature, competitive markets, global and local economics and other dynamic forces constantly create chaos and defy any mathematical formula for success.

Second, they don't realize the simple fact that everything falls into place through proper execution.

My personal instinct is to be an aggressive number cruncher and analyzer. The knowledge contained in numbers is both an indicator of the status of a business and a predictor of things to come. I also advocate well-developed quantitative strategies because they impose the discipline managers need to think several moves ahead instead of being reactive.

Then why do I refer to the practice of management as an art? Because the numbers are the pallet, the strategy is the canvas and strategic implementation is the passion that transform a business into a work of art.

Unfortunately, today's fashion is to seek out and reward managers who paint by the numbers and stay inside the lines. This yields managers who don't see the interaction between light and dark and how they shade the picture. They don't see opportunities to mix colors to create a more vibrant painting. They don't generate the creativity and innovation that inspires more exciting art than they thought possible. And most importantly, painting by the numbers and staying in the lines stifle intelligent risk taking.

The Lost Art of General Management

Basic Skills

The Lost Art of General Management

Chapter 1:
What Is a General Manager?

In This Chapter:

- The View from 40,000 Feet Meets the Subatomic Particle
- A General Manager's Basic Skill Set
  - Why You Have to Know How Your Company Makes Money
  - Why You Have to Know How Your Customers Make Money
  - How You Can Add Value to Customer Relationships By Understanding the Market
  - Why You Need to Understand How Your Competitors Relate to Your Customers
  - Why You Need to Understand the Industry Beyond Customer Relationships
  - The Importance of Customer Relationships at Multiple Levels
  - Solid Knowledge of Your Company's Other Functional Areas
  - Solid Computer and Internet Skills
  - A Sincere Interest in Developing Your Employees And Yourself

The View from 40,000 Feet Meets the Subatomic Particle

How many people have you met in your career who are equally comfortable viewing the world from 40,000 feet and from up close?

Not many, I'll bet. I'm sure you've worked with people who can see the world from 40,000 feet, but are clueless when it comes to the day-to-day details that can make or break a business. And it's likely you also have met their opposites – the micromanagers who only see minutia. These people can't guide a business because they can't see where it's headed.

The achilles heel that these two, not-so-rare extremes have in common is functional tunnel vision. While they view the world from very different perspectives, they both tend to be strongly biased by their particular work functions.

I can illustrate this point through a construct I developed that uses a targeting site as an analogy. In the following diagram, the X-axis is the "perspective axis" and the Y-axis is the "functional axis." Managers who want to hit their targets need to aim in the crosshairs. When they are drawn to any of the corners, they are bound to miss their target.

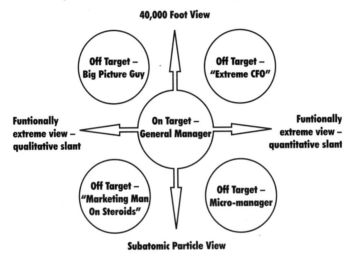

I use the term "general manager" to refer to people who are equally comfortable at 40,000 feet, right up close and all points in between. In short, these are the managers who make it their business to get to know how their business operates beyond the boundaries of their departments or divisions.

Because they understand their businesses from high altitudes as well as through the microscope of their daily jobs, true general managers understand how actions taken in one functional area impact all the other areas of the business.

More importantly, they understand how to put this knowledge to work, helping to steer the business along a successful course.

I chose the title "The Lost Art of General Management" for this book because it truly is an art. If business were essentially a science – the pursuit of predictable patterns of causes and effects – the Dow would be at 50,000. But business can be approached from many different directions with countless ideas and strategies, which is why it requires the instincts of a general manager.

General management has become a lost art for many reasons, including the emergence of large, functionally segmented companies; the dot com/dot bomb evolution; a decade of economic expansion and hundreds of "magic bullet" business books that have relegated it to the subconscious of business think.

The art of general management must reemerge before we can get the economy and the stock market off the sandbar the current captains of industry have beached them on. Executives in all business disciplines can help lead the way, even though they are the most likely practitioners of functional myopia and magic-bullet solutions.

A General Manager's Basic Skill Set

Do you have the basic skill set of a general manager? How many of these things do you use every day at work?

- an understanding of how your company makes money
- an understanding of how *your customers* make money
- an understanding of the market (necessary to add value to customer relationships)
- an understanding of how your competitors relate to the customers
- an understanding of the industry beyond customer relationships
- customer relationships at multiple levels
- solid technical knowledge of your company's processes
- solid computer and Internet skills
- a sincere interest in developing your employees and yourself

General managers rely on all these skills to ensure their efforts are directed towards helping their company meet its overall objectives.

In this chapter we will review these basic skill sets. In the chapters that follow, we will address the more advanced skills required to become a full-fledged general manager.

Why You Have to Know How Your Company Makes Money

This seems like a silly topic. Of course you know how your company makes money and that it needs to make money to survive.

But I'd be willing to bet you need to take a deeper look. Your value to the company is directly tied to the depth of your understanding of how it makes money. If your reaction to the previous paragraph was something like, "we make ladders, so we make money by selling ladders," you're not seeing the whole picture.

In the steel- or drywall-manufacturing businesses, for instance, high-capacity utilization is how money is made. Production volume is critical because, while factories represent huge capital investments, they generate relatively low-margin products.

By contrast, management-consulting firms can make money without running at full capacity. Their "machinery" is people, and since salaries are a relatively low overhead expense compared to the fees they charge, these companies prefer to be overstaffed if that means they're able to respond to more urgent (and profitable) consulting opportunities.

Most companies fall somewhere between these extremes. The important thing is to realize that your everyday decisions send ripples throughout the company that impact volume, costs and pricing. Unless you know how to prioritize those three things in the context of your business, you can't be an effective general manager.

This first precept is so important that we drill down deeper into how companies make money in the next chapter.

Why You Have to Know How Your Customers Make Money

It's a simple question and a simple concept, but how many people really understand how their customers make money?

Why is it important? For one reason, because people who understand how their customers make money are better able to design their marketing approaches and other communications in ways that respond to their customers' particular needs.

But it cuts deeper than sales and marketing. Once you appreciate how your customers make money, you may find it necessary to adapt your products, services and financial terms to meet their needs. By establishing a pattern of responsiveness in this fashion, a business develops stronger ties to its customers. By adding tangible value to relationships (and nothing's more tangible than helping your customer generate cash and earn profits), an affinity is created that can prevent customers from jumping ship at the first sign of trouble with your products or services.

It is critical to understand the customer's internal processes to assure that your company's business processes (such as customer service) are well connected to the customer. Visiting a customer's facilities, plants, retail outlets, etc. helps facilitate the process of getting to know how your customer makes money.

Real World Story No. 1

The various building-materials businesses I have worked for serve customers who run the gamut from "mom & pop" operations to large national buying groups and "big-box" retailers such as Lowe's and Home Depot.

All the companies I worked for manufactured *commodity* building materials, meaning that there was little to distinguish our products from our competitors' products. Our strategy was to differentiate ourselves through our go-to-market efforts – approaching each segment differently – even though we sold them all identical products.

The mom & pops tend not to worry about large profits. They're mainly interested in stripping free cash flow from the business and avoiding as much personal income tax as the law allows. With these folks, our goal was to show them how we could reduce their inventory (not tie cash up in inventory), offer them special payments (permit them to hold their money longer) and pay incentive rebates quarterly or monthly instead of yearly (expediting the payment of interest-free incentive dollars).

Of course, we had to factor all this into our cost. Consequently, the mom & pops paid a higher price – which may have reduced their profits a bit, but it sure sped up their cash flow!

A large national buying cooperative on the other hand needs to demonstrate to its members that the supplier relationships it negotiates on their behalf bring value. Businesses that join buying cooperatives generally want to be able to buy at a better price. This is because their main interest is turning larger profits so they can grow and compete against larger competitors in their market.

Therefore, our strategy with "buy-groups" was to offer highly incentivized rebate programs linked to yearly goals. When these goals weren't met (when they didn't buy enough of our product), we reduced the rebates. Until we paid out the rebates, however, we were able to use the money to leverage our cash flow. In turn, we allocated the earnings on those funds back into the pricing structure for the buy groups – further enhancing our competitiveness.

It's much tougher to gain a similar win-win situation with big-box retailers, however. Typically, they seem interested only in win-lose situations in which they're the winner and you're the loser. That would be hard enough to cope with if there were only one big-box retailer, so we realized it was totally unrealistic to keep them all happy.

At one company I worked for, we decided to focus on keeping only one big-box outfit happy – and we selected Lowe's, because for one thing Lowe's fit our geographic coverage better than Home Depot. In fact, we added value to our relationship with Lowe's by partnering with them on a strategy directed against Home Depot.

Big-box retailers are large corporations. Their hot button is the value of their shares. Wall Street evaluates their performance based on two things – how particular stores perform from one year to the next, and the number of new stores they open.

Through our decision to partner with Lowe's, we helped them (in our own little way) improve comp store sales. Just as important, they knew we were ready, willing and more than able to provide them competitive information on new markets since they knew we were linking our success to theirs.

This illustrates why it's important to understand how your customers make money. If we had approached all three customer segments with the same strategy – rebates only, for example – we would have limited the potential for success from the get-go. Instead, we made impressive market-share gains in all three segments.

How You Can Add Value to Customer Relationships By Understanding the Market

It's essential that you become known as an expert in your market. Once you or your company become the authority that customers and industry associations call to find out about current and future trends, you've claimed a position of leadership that sets you apart from your competitors – both on the corporate and personal levels.

Most people don't have the time or the inclination to analyze, theorize and interpret all the factors that influence the maturation of a given industry. If they did, there wouldn't be thousands of consultants out there charging huge fees to provide that exact service. Once *you* become the expert, however, you can provide your insight to customers and potential customers for "free!"

For significantly less than the cost of consulting fees, your company can hire an MBA from an average school with some real-world experience. An in-house MBA is pretty cheap when compared to consultants' fees in the $50,000 – $100,000 range each time you need a study done.

But the value of this MBA is measured in more than consulting fees avoided. Your resident market analyst can skyrocket the value your customers see in doing business with you and help cement relationships.

Real World Story No. 2

A large buying co-op asked me to update them on developments in one segment of the building-materials industry by making a presentation at one of their meetings.

Because the coop's chairperson was concerned that I would turn the presentation into a hour-long infomercial for my company, he kept calling to remind me that the presentation *really, really* needed to be about the industry at large, not just about my firm. I kept reassuring him I would honor his request.

In preparing for the presentation, I gathered the collective wisdom of our company on all segments of the industry. I also researched trade associations, periodicals and the Internet. Then I enlisted the help of several people to boil it down to a cohesive and comprehensive treatise on the industry as it directly pertained to the cooperative's members.

It was a lot of work but it paid off. After the presentation, many delegates asked me questions, so I hung around for a second hour talking to them one-on-one. To a person, all said they wanted to do business with us. The upshot was, I was invited to speak at three of the member firms' management meetings – with the same result.

Based on the business we derived from this activity, my presentation *had been* an hour-long infomercial for my company. But it wouldn't have happened unless I had been prepared to present myself as an expert in the building-materials industry.

Why You Need to Understand How Your Competitors Relate to Your Customers

The marketplace is dynamic – always changing, always moving. There are no constants and everything is a variable. *Competition* is one of the variables that cause flux in the marketplace.

Each competitor approaches its customers in one of five standardized ways:

1. As a leader
2. As a follower
3. As a revolutionary
4. As a stabilizer
5. As a reactionary participant

Which one of these five types do your customers perceive your company to be?

The reality is that unless your company combines the characteristics of a leader and a revolutionary, the sales and marketing function will not be able to influence the company's success. An effective general manager has the perspective to realize the importance of this image, and ensures that the company is perceived accordingly.

A follower is in a weaker position. The leader is always dictating the rules and the price. Followers are always on the defensive and at the mercy of customers who shop their prices and programs among competitors as leverage for negotiating better deals.

Stabilizers are competitors who want to get the competitive landscape into equilibrium; leaving a little room for everyone, and hoping to squeeze out a little extra margin for themselves. This may be a noble intent but it's not a great strategy because stabilizers can never prevent leaders from moving in new directions.

Stabilizers also are potential victims of the reactionary participant; irrational competitors who jump to match any price movement whether or not the move is consistent with their overall market position. The reactionary participant is typically the weakest competitor in a market – the one in the greatest danger of being squeezed out. There is one in every market.

Being the leader doesn't necessarily require the largest share, the broadest product line or the most innovative products in a market segment. The competitor that sets the go-to-market strategy that customers prefer and creates price leadership – the same competitor everyone is targeting – is the leader in any segment.

Quite often, the largest player in a market deludes itself by thinking it's also the leader. In fact, it may have been the leader before complacency led to resting on laurels and losing the ability to truly understand the dynamics of their ever-changing market.

The evolutionary changes that have occurred at Sears and Wal-Mart provide the most remarkable example. Wal-Mart, the world's largest retailer and the largest company in America, was the subject of jokes at Sears' Chicago headquarters not all that long ago.

When Wal-Mart acted like a leader in smaller geographic markets and introduced its revolutionary approach, Sears dismissed it as an upstart that it soon would crush with its superior retailing skills and buying power. But by gaining expertise and momentum in secondary rural markets, Wal-Mart grew its influence before Sears took it very seriously.

This strategy enabled Wal-Mart to hone its craft in retailing, logistics and purchasing and led the retail industry into a new direction with big-box stores.

Why You Need to Understand the Industry Beyond Customer Relationships

Although many businesses position themselves as meeting the full range of their customers' needs, the truth is most of them sell only a portion of what the customer needs. Personal computers are a good example. Who sells a total hardware and software package? No one. Who supplies Wal-Mart all of its products? No one. Who supplies GM all of its parts? No one.

Consequently, doesn't it stand to reason that companies that don't compete with yours directly still can impact your market and customers? For example, let's say your company supplies plastic parts to the automotive industry. Your supply chain is full, but you see that a shortage of sheet steel will be slowing auto production. Does it make better business sense to continue manufacturing plastic components at the same rate, or to begin scaling back in anticipation of reduced demand from automakers? Should you consider developing special discounts to customers who keep their purchasing levels up?

If you were ahead of the curve, you would be working with a few critical steel suppliers and learning which auto manufacturers they planned to allocate their steel to. Then, you would follow in their wake and pick up business as you go.

By understanding your customers' universe (their supply chains) you can take advantage of adjacencies you otherwise would never consider. You should get to know all your customers' key suppliers and forge a strategic network with them.

Real World Story No. 3

When I was working in South America, I was in the acoustical ceiling tile business ... or so I thought.

I was out there selling building material distributors on why they needed to be in the ceiling tile business. Sales were growing, but not at the rate I thought they could.

Because I actively listened to what I was hearing from these distributors – the leaders in South America – I began to realize that they were actually selling "dry construction" techniques. The old-line distributors, on the other hand, were selling products into the status quo market – the "wet construction" segment consisting of block, concrete, plaster, etc.

The cutting-edge distributors were selling materials associated with construction that is more like the way things are done in the States. So, rather than try to sell a distributor ceiling tiles *per se*, it made sense to help the distributor advance the cause of using dry construction techniques to South America's major developers of office and retail buildings and hotels.

To this end, we formed alliances with drywall, insulation and steel-framing producers. We coordinated our efforts to sell dry construction techniques in the same market. Calling jointly on architects, banks (they provide the financing for building development) and contractors – in addition to the developers.

We were able to convert enough projects to dry construction in just one year that our ceiling tile business grew in excess of 155 percent. More importantly, operating profit grew more than 400 percent.

Why did operating profits grow so much? Because we were able to charge more for the value we delivered once we convinced the market that the speed of dry construction reduces its cost.

Before customers converted to dry construction, we had to discount our product to get people to try it. When they did try it, they struggled with installation and the need to coordinate it with the rest of a wet construction project. Consequently, we could only charge what the product was perceived to be ... which wasn't much.

The Importance of Customer Relationships At Multiple Levels

Did you ever work with a financial planner or stockbroker you liked who changed firms? Did you follow him or her from firm A to firm B? I bet you did.

You did so because your trust and your relationship were rooted in that one person, not with the brokerage as an entity. After all, business is simply people doing business with other people. This explains why firms like Merill Lynch have been known to pay astronomical retention packages to their key financial advisors. The cost of lost business is much greater than a salary increase.

Real World Story No. 4

I was using a financial services firm whose vice president would call me now and again instead of relying only on the junior planner who worked with me from month to month. This VP would shake my hand on my semi-annual visits and occasionally take me to lunch. He put the emphasis on "above and beyond" activity to build the relationship with me.

I learned that he spent most of his time with clients in this way. Why? Because his strategy was to let the less experienced younger talent brings the clients in, then make sure he hung onto the clients when those junior talents got lured away by his competitors.

It worked. When the terrific young professional I worked with took off, the VP was on the phone to me before the younger guy moved into his new office and had a chance to fire up his Palm Pilot. The VP assigned me to a new rookie and I was OK with that because I knew I had access to the VP if I had a problem or concern, or just wasn't happy with my new planner.

I've seen the same thing in the building-materials industry when a hot sales executive has left to work for a competitor and taken most of his customers with her or him.

It actually can cut both ways. If a purchasing agent has invested time in developing personal relationships with suppliers, those relationships will be maintained if he or she moves to a new firm. That's why it's important to make sure your company's relationships with its customers are solid on many levels.

The goal is to get multiple connection points so if one of those connections is lost or strained, the relationship with the customer is still maintained. You don't have to have someone quit for the one-person connection to bite you. Relationships get strained now and again. It's important to have those other ties to help you through the difficult times.

Multiple connection points also improve two-way communications, providing more information and more insight into the needs of customers. Because they serve as an effective feedback loop, multiple connections can also help you learn about problems before they get too large.

Solid Knowledge of Your Company's Other Functional Areas

If your company makes ladders, do you know how the ladders are made? If your company is a management consulting firm, do you know how your company gains clients or manages projects?

Most people understand their own functional processes within their company but not how the rest of the company works. If you work for a large multinational in the IT department, should you care what the manufacturing or accounting departments do?

Absolutely. After all, IT touches everything. By understanding how your company really functions, you can do your job better. You're the one that understands your function best; by understanding the other functions, you're better equipped to be a better internal partner.

The best Human Resources person I had the pleasure of working with once stood up at a meeting of our company's worldwide HR managers and stopped it dead. He stopped it because he kept hearing attendees refer to the company's employees as "customers." They kept talking about the need to get to know these "customers" better.

The HR manager knew this philosophy is far too internally focused, and he made it clear that it was the people and organizations who bought our products – and only those people and organizations – who *truly* were our customers.

Then he explained that he had taken the trouble to educate himself as to the needs of our actual customers and had spent time getting to know them. I called him the best HR person I've worked with because he helped me hire and train more than 20 sales people in less than a year. He had an eye for the kind of person who would succeed in selling to our real customers. Because he had a better understanding of our sales people, he *was* better able to service their HR needs.

Getting to know your company's other functions some-times requires getting some dirt under your fingernails. If you work for a manufacturing company, spend time on the factory floor. Whatever your company does, roll your sleeves up and become "hands-on" in other functional processes as a general course of training.

Solid Computer and Internet Skills

In this day in age, why should I have to point out the im-portance of learning how to fully use a personal computer? When I joined my most recent company, I attended a sales meeting where a new CRM (Customer Relationship Manage-ment) system was being rolled out. When the trainer told the group to double click on the CRM icon on their laptops, *three* sales people raised their hands and asked what "double-click" meant!

It still amazes me that many people who graduated from high school prior to 1985 still only use their laptops for e-mail.

With the billions spent on information technology, it's also amazing that more companies don't make sure their people have the skills to take full advantage of the true power of the information age. More surprising is the number of people who don't make it their business to become more valuable by learning computer skills on their own.

"Data mining" is an important tool for adding value to your customer relationship by improving your understanding of the market. The data comes from your company's systems and from the Internet. Since many of your customers don't have the computer savvy to engage in data mining, you can use it to strengthen your relationships with them while adding to your value on the job.

A Sincere Interest in Developing Your Employees And Yourself

According to General Colin Powell, "Organization doesn't really accomplish anything. Plans don't accomplish anything, either. Theories of management don't much matter. Endeavors succeed or fail because of the people involved. Only by at-tracting the best people will you accomplish great deeds."

I couldn't agree more. While it's essential to attract the best people, they also have to be developed. Too often, managers undervalue their people, considering them not smart enough to "get it," or viewing them as dead wood. On the other hand, there are managers who value their people but just don't realize they have to develop them... or are afraid to address developmental issues.

Like the precept of understanding how your company makes money, we also will drill down on this later in the book. Let's face it, if you understand how your company really makes money and you attract and develop the best people, there are no limits on how far you can lead it. The ability to develop people is the essence of true leadership.

Just as important as developing your people is developing yourself. The bar is raised every year. What are you doing to hone and develop your skills in order to clear the bar every year? Reading this book is one step. Executive education at key universities is another that I recommend.

In order to determine what areas need improvement, actively solicit feedback from your boss, peers and subordinates. This is a positive, proactive step in identifying areas that need improvement and gaps in your skills.

Chapter 2:
The Purpose of a Business

In This Chapter:

- Success Is Nothing to be Ashamed Of
- Generating Cash Is Not the Same as Generating Profit

Before you can fully understand what a general manager is and what it takes to be a general manager, you first have to understand the purpose of a business. The purpose of a business is extremely simple – which is probably why it's often overlooked.

The purpose of all businesses is the same whether they're Fortune 500 companies, management consulting firms or corner hardware stores. That may seem surprising. How can Microsoft and Joe's Hardware have the same underlying business purpose?

Simply because the purpose of *any* business is to (a) generate cash and (b) earn a profit.

Without a positive cash flow (generating cash), no business can survive for long. And unless it is profitable, no business can attract the capital it needs for growth, or provide for its owners and employees.

At the grassroots level, business is nothing more than providing goods and services in exchange for money. That's why it can be said that Microsoft and the corner hardware store have the same purpose.

Many people are apt to confuse a business' vision or mission with its purpose. They forget that it must generate cash and earn a profit in order to achieve its vision. We'll cover vision and mission issues in a later chapter

Success Is Nothing to Be Ashamed Of

Generating cash and earning a profit are not about greed. Generating cash and earning a profit are not why the accounting scandals of 2001 and 2002 occurred. In fact, the opposite is true – they occurred at companies that *couldn't* generate sufficient cash and profits.

These firms lacked leaders who thought and acted like general managers. What they *did* have, however, were leaders who didn't really understand their businesses and were not involved for the sake of the business to begin with. Personal greed and get-rich-quick schemes are not qualities I associate with general managers.

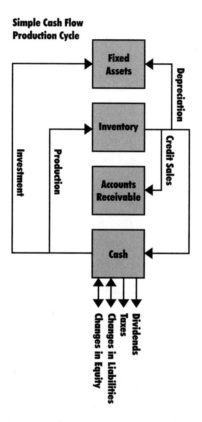

Simple Cash Flow Production Cycle

Generating Cash Is Not the Same as Generating Profit

A company runs on cash generated from operations, debt and investment. Without cash to meet its current expenses and run its operations, a company is bankrupt.

It's important to note that generating positive cash flow is not the same as generating a profit. Neither does positive cash flow *guarantee* a profit. Just because a company may be pulling in more cash than it's putting out doesn't mean that it's making money. If a business is unprofitable, it needs to get back to profitability quickly before the cash begins to flow in the other direction.

The following Q&A should help clarify a few other aspects of basic business finance:

Q. *How can a business have a positive cash flow but not be profitable?*

A. Easy – positive cash flow only means that a business is taking in more cash than it's putting out.

Collecting money from customers sooner than creditors need to be paid is one way that positive cash flow happens. Bank loans can also cover current cash gaps. If a business is not profitable, it must devise a plan to get profitable before cash flow turns negative. When cash flow turns negative, a business becomes a "dead man walking" unless it has other options at its disposal for generating cash.

More businesses close or seek bankruptcy protection not because they are unprofitable but because they aren't generating a positive cash flow. Rapid business growth without the appropriate cash plan often leads to this. Also, highly leveraged businesses that hit a slump in revenues due to economic downturns also can get caught in the cash trap.

While the concept of cash flow is easy to understand, it is more difficult to practice. Business risks must be taken, albeit intelligent risks. To expand and make more money, businesses need to invest. These investments can be funded by cash on hand, debt or the floating of equity. Regardless of the purpose, however, cash will be tight for a period of time before the investment begins to pay off. This is why virtually all businesses have credit lines they can draw on when they require funds during such periods.

The bottom line: you need to understand how cash flows and how to manage it.

Q. *Yes, but I'm a middle manager at a large multinational company. How do I manage cash flow?*

A. The cash monster still needs to be fed regardless of how big or small a company is. What influence do you have in terms of your company's receivables or payables? Do you authorize any expenses? Do you manage any inventories? Are you involved with sales? If you answered "yes" to any of these questions, you can influence cash flow!

Positive cash flow is important to any size or type of business, not just as a matter of survival, but as a source of *free financing*. Think about it. If you have more cash coming in than going out, can't you use some of those funds to pay off debt, invest in equipment or enter new markets?

Q. *Isn't making a profit just a simple matter of selling product for a higher price than your total cost?*

A. Yes, it is, but do you know what your total costs *really* are? Should you factor in opportunity cost? By the way, what *is* opportunity cost?

Let's look at each of these questions.

How to determine what total costs really are:

One would normally consider this an easy question for any business to answer, but often it isn't. Many larger firms use standard costs as a basis of measurement, which is a rather antiquated way at looking at costs. Standard costs are based on a budget of what a business thinks its costs will be. Variance reports are generated at the end of each month to determine how the actual costs deviated from the standard. While this is all well and good, things such as allocations, unforeseen swings in the cost of raw materials and changes in unit volumes can render this nothing more than a theoretical exercise.

Smarter companies look at their costs in a more dynamic sense. Instead of relying on standard costs, they establish working models that can be used to assess the impact of volume growth or shrinkage, pricing fluctuations, purchasing costs and more.

While there is no one perfect method for viewing costs, businesses need to firmly grasp how changes in volume, price and material costs impact their bottom line. For example, if a customer offers you an opportunity to get a much larger share of their business, but you have to discount your product in order to get that volume, how much can you reduce the price and still make the deal worth it for you?

As you can see from the following table, if you reduce your price to $93/widget, you would be better off taking the order at the lower volume of 1,000 units and the higher price of $100. Alarmingly, however, most sales people won't take the time to

Selling Price Of Widget	Cost of Widget	Margin	Units Sold	Profit
$100	$80	$20	1,000	$20,000
$93	$80	$13	1,500	$19,500

do this simple math. When a customer says they'll buy 50 percent more if the price is cut, sales people reflexively ask, "How much do I need to cut my price?"

While we're on the subject of costs, I've found that managers tend to overlook the critical need to understand how payment terms affect their cost. Cash discounts are a cost that needs to be monitored. Length of receivable terms directly affects cash flow and is part of opportunity costs.

In its simplest form, opportunity cost is the difference between the amount you make doing what you're doing, and the amount you *could make* if you were doing something else.

Receivable terms constitute an opportunity cost when they allow a business' customers to hang onto their money for longer and longer periods and prevent the business from using the same funds for its own purposes. That's why companies offer discounts for faster payment. It's often cheaper for the seller to discount its goods and get paid faster than wait longer to receive full payment.

EVA® or Economic Value Added truly focuses on opportunity costs. The concept behind EVA is that a company or a division creates value for its owners only when its operating income exceeds the cost of capital employed. EVA is an opportunity-cost analysis of the activity of the whole company or division.

The formula for EVA is: EVA = EBIT(1 – Tax Rate) – KwC

Where: EBIT(1 – Tax Rate) = after-tax operating income

Kw = weighted average cost of capital

C = the capital employed by creditors and owners (shareholders or investors)

KwC therefore represents an annual capital charge.

Opportunity costs should always be factored into pricing decisions.

Your accounting methodology can greatly affect how you view your cost. FIFO and LIFO present a good case in point. FIFO-based inventory costs assume that the First goods In are the First goods Out. LIFO assumes the opposite – that the Last goods in are the First to go out.

At a steel-forming company I worked for, a huge gyration of the price in steel came into play. The price of the steel we were receiving from the mills increased between 60 and 70 percent in just a few months.

There's normally an interval of from three to five months between the time steel-forming companies order coils of steel from a steel mill and they ship products made from that steel. However, our customers dealt with us in a shorter time frame. The normal lead time between order and shipment normally ranged between two days and two weeks, which required us to maintain large inventories of unfinished steel to meet customer-service expectations.

When we were hit with these price increases, we immediately instituted a price increase in the market. Needless to say, our sales organization was concerned about this move. At first, many of our competitors would not follow; they told their customers that they were still buying steel at a great price. Our sales organization was in a panic because they thought we had been taken by the mills and were at competitive disadvantage. I made my sales people stick to their guns and quote the higher prices. But I also committed my company to honoring the higher prices for the long run.

Again, more anguish from the field. But lo and behold, one day our competitors not only published massive price increases, they also rescinded many quotes.

Why did they do this? Well, they were apparently on a FIFO basis of accounting, so their sales people were only seeing the cost of steel as reported by their accounting departments. The people running the sales organization apparently didn't understand that their costs were going to explode once the cheaper steel was taken off the books in the FIFO method.

While we may have looked a little opportunistic to our customers at first, they quickly saw that betting on us was better because we could tell them what was going to happen to their price more accurately than the competition. This gave them the ability to better manage their costs and cash flow.

Anyone not trained in finance or accounting should take an executive education course in finance for non-financial managers. If your employer doesn't pay for it, consider it an investment in yourself as per the ninth skill we described in Chapter 1, "A Sincere Interest in Developing Your Employees and Yourself."

Strategic Skills

The Lost Art of General Management

Chapter 3:
The Strategy Behind Strategy

In This Chapter:

- What Is Strategy?
- Mission Statements
- The Vision Thing
  - Lack of Vision
  - Feel-Good Vision
  - Focused Vision
  - Personal Vision
- Development of a Strategic Hypothesis
- Testing the Hypothesis
- Implementation and Execution of the Strategy
- Tuning the Strategy as Circumstances Warrant

What Is Strategy?

Strategy is a unique game plan designed to gain a position in a specific market. It is unique because it takes advantage of a company's specific strengths while minimizing or neutralizing its weaknesses and exploiting the weaknesses of its competitors.

This is easy to say but very hard to do. Strategy development is complex because markets are fluid; they change rapidly and they change all the time. This is what the military refers to as the "fog of war."

However dense the fog, a plan does need to be developed, tested, implemented and revised as circumstances dictate. As I see it, there are six steps in developing a business strategy:

1. Development of a concise mission statement
2. Articulating a clear vision
3. Developing a hypothesis of how to achieve that vision
4. Testing and revision of the hypothesis
5. Implementing and executing the strategy (the outcome of the hypothesis)
6. Tuning the strategy as circumstances warrant

Mission Statements

Many companies spend tens of thousands of dollars hiring consulting firms to help them develop a mission statement. I don't necessarily think this is a wise investment. A mission statement is simply a description of the ballpark you want to play in. Do you need a baseball diamond or a football grid-iron? A mission statement is not much more than a description of the overall purpose of your company, division or department.

Don't be concerned if your definition doesn't exactly fit the textbook definitions touted by consulting firms. And don't make the mistake of overcomplicating your mission state-ment... too much sophistication will kill your statement.

Here is an example of a simple mission statement:

"We will be a leading provider of widgets to the big-box retailer. We will establish our leadership through service, in-tegrity and ingenuity in meeting our customer's needs."

This hastily drawn mission statement tells you the product segment, customer segment or channel and the seed of the strategy to accomplish the mission (of service). With this kind of mission statement for the company at large, each depart-ment can develop its own that ties to the overarching mis-sion. This now becomes the platform for developing a *vision* statement that will describe in detail how the mission will be carried out.

The Vision Thing

The expression "the vision thing" was coined by George H.W. Bush, who explained that he lacked "the vision thing" during his 1992 re-election campaign. The absence of the vision thing, he said, was largely responsible for losing to Bill Clinton.

The vision thing has done more harm than good to com-panies over the last 20 years, in my opinion. It has done more harm than good because companies cannot seem to find a middle road to focus on. Either they don't have a vision, and are therefore condemned to wander aimlessly wherever the winds take them – or they have an esoteric, politically correct, feel-good, public relations-driven thing they call their "vision," but that provides no direction.

Before a company can develop a strategy, it must articulate a vision for itself. The vision that will guide and focus the business must address three questions:

1. Who are we?
2. Where are we going?
3. How are we going to get there?

A vision needs to be *exclusive* rather than *inclusive*... this is the essence of focus. If the vision includes too much in an effort to be all things to all people, it will become unwieldy – or worse, meaningless. Including too much in a vision is probably the single biggest mistake that companies make when drafting a vision statement.

The vision must, however, include the business' core competencies.

Lack of Vision

I've heard intelligent presidents and CEOs say they don't want to state a vision because it could be too confining. They don't want their people to miss business opportunities that don't obviously link to the company's stated vision.

I've always assumed this means one of two things: Either the leader is copping out because he or she lacks vision, or the leader truly believes the statement and doesn't understand that the lack of vision *ensures* a lack of focus.

After three hours of searching www.annualreportservice.com (a web site of annual reports for all publicly traded companies on the NYSE, NASDAQ and AMEX), I found very few companies that actually publish a vision or mission statement – or even a specific set of goals. Typically, they just give a brief overview of the business they're in.

Managers are faced with countless decisions every day that can steer the company left or right of their intended course. A clearly articulated vision is like a compass; it helps steer decision making in the direction the company has planned to go.

Yogi Berra once said, "If you don't know where you are going, you might not get there." As usual, he was absolutely right.

Feel-Good Vision

When developing their vision statements, large publicly traded companies typically fall into the trap of settling for "feel-good" visions. Corporate staffers such as public relations or shareholder relations professionals take what the business wants as a vision and obscure it into something so benign and "happy" that it means nothing.

Their priority is ensuring the company will be perceived as being all things to all people. The public relations folks write the vision to neutralize any pressure groups they may be forced to deal with, such as local community or environmental groups who oppose their projects.

Sometimes, however, executives have nobody to blame but themselves. Having practiced the marketing profession, I know how easy it is to be drawn to creating visions that sound intellectual but are nothing more than overly complex.

After a group of marketing executives gets its hands on the vision and modifies it, you're left with something like this:

- "Our mission is to build businesses that inform and entertain our customers in the ways, places and at times they want."

That's a fairly broad vision! While anyone would agree that companies have to be careful to avoid defining themselves too narrowly, mission statements like the above offer nothing to focus on. What's more, a vision statement doesn't have to last forever or be an all-defining goal. The CEO should always be looking to what the business should or can be in the future, and have the latitude to change the vision as appropriate.

Here's another interesting vision statement:

- "Our vision is to realize a future where ingenuity and commitment can redefine what's possible in the automotive industry. This is the opportunity for GM: Imagine it. We have the ability, the resources and the drive to achieve it."

What in this vision tells you who GM is, where it's going or how it plans to get there? As a customer, how would you react to this? As an investor, does this vision raise your comfort level? As an employee, does this vision help you focus on the critical few things you need to achieve at work?

Here's a vision statement that's even vaguer, if that's a word:
- "Our products will heighten the beauty and safety of buildings everywhere."

What business is this company in? Is there a new business category called the "floral and fire extinguisher" segment? Is it in the non-combustible fabrics business? You wouldn't know it from their vision statement, but the company operates in a narrow segment of the building materials industry.

I can assure you from insider knowledge this vision led to thousands of lost decision-making hours each year, not to mention millions of dollars lost in research and development and through failed ventures involving business lines the company had no business entering. But those businesses were consistent with the company's vision statement.

Real World Story No. 6

A building products company I worked for formed a Global Marketing Team to develop filters (also known as a "screener") to help get the company focused. People traveled worldwide to attend quarterly meetings for the purpose of selecting the filters.

Each meeting was characterized by arguments over the proper method of evaluating projects. Screener after screener was developed to filter down all the projects that were proposed from all over the world. It was obvious to me that the reason we couldn't develop an effective screener was that we didn't have a vision of who we were. We were operating in an information vacuum into which poured confusion, politics and the inevitable "idea of the day" projects.

Focused Vision

Real World Story No. 7

Contrast that with my experience at the gypsum division of a large diversified building materials company. When I joined the company, it had just installed a new CEO of the global gypsum business. He said we had to get focused – and he was right. Gypsum can be used to make lots of products, from drywall and floor screeds to dental fillings and food additives.

Although our division was primarily in the drywall segment, its various operations around the world were dabbling with all the other uses of gypsum. While some folks believed the gypsum business should be all-encompassing, the new CEO realized that the global business lacked focus as a result. Worse, he saw that it was slowing the company's forward progress.

In order to get his strategy in order, he decided to institute a new vision. After collaborating with his key reports, he released the new vision: "We will be the world leader in drywall and associated systems."

He explained that an "associated system" was anything that touched drywall and would enable us to sell more drywall.

He went on further to define what it meant to be a world leader:

1. Have the low net delivered cost position.
2. Be the benchmark for product innovation.
3. Offer the widest geographic coverage.

With this vision, it was easy to define who we were, where we were going and how we were going to get there. Nothing fancy, nothing flowery, nothing sophisticated or cerebral. But you really understood the game plan.

Nailing "the vision thing" doesn't *guarantee* success, either. The strategy for "how we are going to get there" has to be properly developed and well-executed to succeed. The vision thing is the first step, so it's essential to get it right. The vision charts the course for the balance of your journey.

If your company doesn't have a vision, you should develop one for your area of influence. You don't have to make any grand pronouncements, just sit with people and decide "who we are, where we're going and how we're going to get there." You'll be pleased with the impact this exercise will have on results.

Personal Vision

Do you have a personal vision? This has to be different from your personal goals, such as "my vision is to be president by the time I'm 35," or "my vision is to earn seven figures." A personal vision needs to address the simple "who, where and how."

You probably read my vision for this book in the Introduction. I have shared with you my background and experience (who I am). I shared with you that I wanted to pass along the mentoring that I was fortunate enough to receive in my career so that readers can discover and utilize the lost art of general management to enhance and grow their professional careers (where we are going). And then I stated the premise of this book – which is, that managers who take the time to understand the big picture not only are better able to manage their own functions, but also are seen as providing significantly greater value to their employers (how we're going to get there).

There's an ancient Chinese proverb you should keep in mind; "A journey of a thousand miles starts by taking the first step." Make sure you know where you are stepping!

Development of a Strategic Hypothesis

A company's hypothesis needs to define the market the company wants to participate in. This definition should be both quantitative and qualitative.

The quantitative component describes its size, where the market is located and its growth curve (up, down or flat). The qualitative description, based on quantitative analysis, describes the attractiveness of the market and its future. Additionally, it should address potential problems to be avoided.

Here's an example:

"The widget market in the United States is 12 billion units per annum as of 2002. The widget market is primarily located in the Southwest and Northeast, with strong pockets of sales in the Midwest on a seasonal basis. The widget market has outpaced the overall growth in the economy since widgets replaced gadgets as a superior alternative.

It is for this reason that we believe the widget market will continue its strong growth pattern over the next five years. While the margins for widgets are beginning to decline, we believe that we can earn higher than average margins due to our proprietary gadget-making technology, which will provide us with a low-cost position when applied to the production of widgets.

Inasmuch as widgets are an attractive market, more and more competitors are entering. Therefore, it is critical to continue to develop innovative new products to stay ahead of the competition as well as to assure that we continue development of new production technologies that reduce the cost of manufacture in order to maintain our low cost position.

This is a significant shift in strategy for us, since we have primarily been a gadget manufacturer. We will have to take share quickly since we will be speeding the cannibalization of our own products. Fortunately, the channel to market for widgets is the same channel as gadgets, so we will be able to leverage existing customer relationships to speed our entry."

These four paragraphs say a lot. A significant amount of diligence will have to go into the testing of this hypothesis.

Testing the Hypothesis

Many companies utilize consultants to develop vision statements and strategic hypotheses. While consultants certainly can help them focus and offer fresh semi-impartial advice, I don't think it's smart to rely exclusively on consultants to test a hypothesis. Testing of a hypothesis is also a readiness assessment of the organization's ability to execute the strategy. The testing phase will flush out internal objections to the plan and organizational barriers to instituting the plan.

More importantly, only the company's actual employees have the industry experience to really put the hypothesis to the test. Your people are actually more impartial in this case than the consultant, who has a vested interest in proving his or her theory is correct. If your people aren't part of the process, it's unrealistic to expect them to take responsibility and accept accountability. They will be less motivated to execute the plan and more motivated to redevelop the plan on the fly.

To illustrate my point, a study by Dr. Eric Siegel, adjunct faculty at the Wharton School of Business, attempted to identify specific criteria that would predict success for entrepreneurs and their management teams.

The Wharton team evaluated a list of hundreds characteristics ranging from education to temperament. They matched their data against the responses from more than 1,000 entrepreneurs. The study found that, while industry experience certainly isn't a guarantor of success, it is a likely indicator. It also found that advanced education isn't a sure guarantor of success, either – although it certainly has value.

The moral of the story is that a company's seasoned people are probably the most qualified to test its strategic hypotheses.

So how *do you* test a hypothesis? Start with the quantitative number crunching. Actually, I like the term "number munching" because crunching connotes filling out spreadsheets not as the means to an end, but as an end in itself. Number munching, on the other hand, requires digesting the numbers and looking for hidden messages. If the numbers don't taste good when you munch them, that's probably the first sign of a problem. If they taste good, keep eating and see if you get indigestion.

I highly recommend involving one of the company's controllers in this process. A good controller can be your best friend. The good ones can tell you which numbers make a difference, such as production costs, staffing costs, capital requirements, etc.

Pairing up the controller with a good marketing analyst connects the inside with the outside. The marketing analyst needs to quantitatively verify all of the market data in (and implied by) the hypothesis.

The outcome of this analysis should be a five-year *pro forma* profit-and-loss statement broken down by quarter. This will serve as the financial road map that will be constantly used to ensure you remain on course during the execution of the strategy.

If the *pro forma* P&L doesn't look good, don't blame it on the quantitative guys trying to kill a good plan. Instead, take an honest look to see if the hypothesis needs to be modified and re-verified quantitatively. It's better to see a problem before the company puts real money on the line and bets its future (and possibly your career) on a bad hypothesis.

I've seen it happen with bright, talented people who fall too deeply in love with their strategic hypotheses. They skip steps in a rush to implementation and dismiss anyone who tries to caution them about roadblocks ahead. In most of the cases where I've witnessed these "car wrecks," the driver only would have needed to steer a little left or a little right, but became too close to their hypothesis to see the road curving in front of them.

Impartial feedback from an independent observer (from another functional discipline or another business unit) can prevent these wrecks.

The qualitative part of testing the hypothesis takes place in the arena of market research. This is where you need to listen to the voice of the customer... and the competitors. You don't have to lay out your strategy to large groups of customers if doing so reveals the cards in your hand before you want to. Learning the gentle art of probing softly with gentle questions will gain you tons of insight into what the channels to market (the customers) think, how they would respond to your strategy, the roadblocks they perceive, and how they envision the future competitive landscape.

Begin by developing a list of questions. The idea is not to directly ask the questions as though you were interrogating customers, but to have in your mind what you want to know when you are out in the field speaking with them. You can set up teams of people in the sales and marketing groups to take on this activity.

It is important to note that this process takes time, particularly if you are trying to keep your plans under wraps. However, if speed is an overwhelming priority, it may be worth investing in the skills of a marketing research consultant. But the marketing research consultant must work closely with your company's internal industry experts to ensure they are going in the right direction and not down blind alleys.

One of the reasons the process takes time is that to really get into the head of the customer, you may need to ask the same questions three times in three different ways. This is what detectives do in trying to get to the truth. Not that your customers will purposefully mislead you, but they may be trying to tell you what they think you want to hear. They could have ulterior motives. Or they just haven't really developed their thoughts yet. It is important to conduct this research at multiple levels within the customer's organization.

By coming at it from three different angles, you will get a clearer picture of the mind of the customer. Once you have this information, you should go back to your quantitative analysis and re-question your numbers based on the market research.

At this point, you will likely have a strategy to achieve the vision. However, you have a decision to make – whether to move into full-fledged implementation or to run a test market or two. This is a good time to check and see if you are still on target, or if a mid-course correction is needed.

If possible, I would suggest that you do a short test market. This is like a dress rehearsal or the preseason in football. You get a chance to see the whole plan come together. You'll spot weaknesses in approach or design that you'll want to adjust.

If circumstances don't allow a test market, you must be prepared to adjust on the fly – and *quickly*.

As you can see, the strategic hypothesis starts with the view from 40,000 feet, while the testing of the hypothesis draws you down closer and closer to ground level until you have the complete picture.

Implementation and Execution of the Strategy

Countdown to launch. Communication is the critical element to implementing and executing any strategy. Your pre-launch checklist should include:

1. A breakdown of responsibilities by function and by name
2. A full understanding by each person, team and function of what is required of them for the implementation
3. A channel for feedback
4. A consistent and clear customer-communications plan.

Once these items are firmly in hand, LAUNCH! The project leader must be in the field to ensure the strategy is being implemented and communicated as intended, and that customer feedback is being carefully listened to and analyzed.

If your launch involves manufacturing a product, being in the field will provide faster feedback to the manufacturing folks that fine tuning may be required. Also, the leader should go to the factories (or to any internal support staff) and provide them feedback directly. Remember to provide positive feedback to your people; you will get more out of these internal groups as a result. Educate them about the market. It doesn't matter if your audience is hourly line workers. They, as much as anyone, need to understand how what they do every day impacts the customers. Also, if they understand the importance of their efforts to the company and the customers, it will inspire pride in their work. The implementation phase is a continuation of the testing phase. You always have to be testing your ideas and adjusting accordingly. At this point, however, it is a live-fire test – no rubber bullets here!

Tuning the Strategy as Circumstances Warrant

No strategy ever succeeds without having to be changed. Remember the military's "fog of war?" It can be deceptive. You may not always see things clearly. Testing and evaluating the strategy for flaws and opportunities never ends. One of the measures of a good leader is the ability to change course when necessary.

Real World Story No. 8

I was general manager of a joint venture based in the United Kingdom that produced a metal building product used extensively throughout Western Europe. The joint venture was between a large publicly traded American company and a publicly traded Dutch company. The JV was formed a few years before I took over as the general manager, and it wasn't going well.

The original vision the partners based the JV on was that they could service the three primary market segments from one uniquely equipped factory utilizing new-to-the-world technology. The three market segments were the commodity segment, the semi-custom segment and the fully engineered segment.

The JV's Board of Directors felt the main reason the JV wasn't performing to expectation was poor implementation of the strategy. There were concerns that the new technology was slow to develop and drew too much time and attention away from the business in general. By getting some fresh perspectives and some new management, the Board thought the strategy could be implemented correctly and achieve the results they were expecting. In reality, the various problems in the factory were symptoms of a flawed strategy rather than poor implementation.

By having a factory that was supposed to be a low-cost commodity producer, a responsive customizer and a developer of engineered projects, we ended up being a jack of all trades and master of none. We were the high-cost commodity producer and the poor-quality custom producer.

It became clear to me within six months of becoming the general manager that this strategy wasn't going to work.

The Board didn't agree. It had invested a lot of time and a lot of money into its strategy, and wasn't ready to abandon it. Also, the strategy had been developed by two of the Board members, so there were political obstacles to work around as well.

Fortunately, I brought on board a terrific plant manager who understood the precepts of being an effective general manager. The plant manager and I pressed on behind the scenes developing a new strategic hypothesis to the effect that the company could only be good (and profitable) by focusing on one segment at its one factory. To serve all three segments as best-in-class, the hypothesis said we needed to have three factories focused on specific market segments.

We figured that if we could quantitatively show that casting off the semi-custom and engineered segments (and focusing on the commodity segment, which our factory was best suited to) we could make the JV profitable. We actually proposed shrinking the top line to grow the bottom line!

We sought the help of one of our partner company's vice president-controllers to verify our financial analysis and assemble our *pro forma* P&L.

Also, we began to focus our energies on selling harder into the commodity segment after we instituted some Board-approved minor factory improvements to the commodity equipment. The efforts seemed to work. I had 80 percent of what I needed to make a convincing argument to the owners, and 80 percent is plenty to make a go of it. General Powell recommends that you go with your gut if you have between 40 and 70 percent of what you need to know. He says that you can't get to 100 percent, and trying to get to 90 percent will cost far too much time and money. I was in good shape with 80 percent, but it was still going to be a tough sell.

To accomplish my goal, I went to the CEO of the Dutch partner who truly is a bottom-line driven person. I felt that making my argument on fiduciary responsibility would win him over, and it did.

Next, I took this endorsement to my primary boss, who was a member of the Board. I needed him to carry the other Board members who were tied to the old strategy. I used the fiduciary argument again, along with the fact that I wasn't abandoning the original strategy, just coming at it from a different angle. I argued that while it would take longer to achieve a position in all three segments, we could do it profitably and generate a positive cash flow very quickly by making the changes I was recommending. Again I was successful in gaining agreement and got the approval to press on with a revised strategy.

It was my neck that was 100 percent on the line because it was my strategy rather than the Board's. That sure has a way of focusing the mind on achieving results! But within three months of instituting the new strategy, we had our first profitable month in the JV. I have to admit that this was one of the proudest moments of my entire career to that point.

Once we moved into the implementation phase, I found that I needed to spend most of my time communicating with everybody. We needed to be very focused, and we could not afford to have people guessing. I utilized the "who we are, where are we going, and how are we going to get there" technique to accomplish this.

After we landed some prestigious work, such as *La Defense* in Paris (the French defense department), the Rotterdam Convention Center and various key projects in the United Kingdom and Belgium, I went to the factory to share this success with the production folks. It was a real pleasure for me to see the sense of pride and accomplishment on their faces that came from knowing their handiwork was on display in some of the most prestigious buildings in Europe.

Don't skip this step in your implementation. Celebrate success. Success breeds success. Take the time to enjoy the accomplishments. It makes the job fun for everyone.

From there, we adjusted the strategy further. We were able to add small amounts of semi-customization once the factory was highly stable and positioned to be the low-cost commodity producer.

Rather than spending capital on building two new factories to penetrate the other two segments, we began to look at potential acquisitions that would not only get us the assets we needed, but the expertise we needed as well. We ended up buying out the Dutch partner and formed an "earn out" JV with a Swiss company that excelled in the other two segments.

Strategy can be an elusive and slippery thing to manage. It takes both the view from 40,000 feet and the subatomic particle approach to develop. It takes team thinking and acting like a general manager. And it requires constant, dispassionate evaluation and adjustment.

Chapter 4:
Marketing Is Everyone's Job

In This Chapter:

- The Process of Marketing: Four "Ps" and Two "Cs"
  - Product Strategy
  - Place Strategy
  - Price Strategy
    - Risk Reduction
    - Profit Improvement
    - The Hassle Factor
    - Ego
  - Promotion Strategy
    - Playing to Our Own Egos
    - Promotion That Is Too Subtle
    - Promotion That Overshadows What Is Being Promoted
    - A Few Thoughts on Internet Promotion
  - Customer Strategy
- One More Tool

Warning: DO NOT SKIP THIS CHAPTER! Whether or not you are a sales or marketing professional, DO NOT SKIP THIS CHAPTER!

Why not? Because marketing is *everyone's* job.

"Marketing" is not simply one of many other functional departments; it is a *capability* that needs to be owned and shared throughout an entire company. The marketing department cannot operate in a vacuum, isolated from the rest of the company. It needs to operate in sync with every other function. Every action the marketing department takes has a ripple effect on the rest of the company, like ripples spreading across a pond.

With that said, what *is* marketing, anyway? Marketing is the link between a company and its customers – a link that operates in both directions. And every action a company takes bears on how effectively that link works. Marketing strategy, properly developed and implemented, is not voodoo or smoke and mirrors. Good marketing strategy is based on fact-based analysis and reasoning. Therefore, the development of a good marketing strategy requires knowledge available from many other disciplines – which is what makes marketing everyone's job.

As a manager who thinks and acts like a general manager, you should also think about marketing and related disciplines such as product development and sales. Since marketing is everyone's job, you should at least understand the basic principles of marketing and understand how what you do can impact the success of the company's marketing strategy positively or negatively.

Before you can contribute to the marketing strategy, the marketing folks will have to be comfortable with your working knowledge of the precepts of their profession. Once they are, you may find them coming to you for your input since they may be starving for the information and value your functional knowledge brings to the marketing strategy.

In the last chapter we talked about strategic planning. In terms of the strategic plan, marketing is where the rubber meets the road!

The Process of Marketing – Four "Ps" and Two "Cs"

In typical marketing textbooks, marketing is described as the four Ps: *Product, Place, Price and Promotion.* I like to add two "Cs" to this: *Competition* and *Customers.* I add "Competition" because markets are highly fluid and the implementation of any marketing strategy results in a specific competitive response that cannot be ignored, either in planning or implementation.

In developing and managing each of the four "Ps," it is always important to stop and evaluate the competition. How will your competitors react to your marketing plan? How will you respond – in fact, how *can* you respond – when they do? How can you minimize the effects of your competitors' attacks on your marketing plan?

I add *"Customers"* because strategic account planning must immediately follow development of the four "Ps." Since there can be no business unless there are customers anyway, there's no harm in taking a belt-and-suspenders approach towards customer development.

Let's drill down through the marketing process, bearing the competitor "C" in mind at each step.

Product Strategy

When developing a product strategy for any product or service, there are only three basic offering modes: full-line offerings, niche or specialty offerings and customized offerings.

In developing your product strategy, you must consider not just the marketing opportunity, but also the competitive set you're dealing with. Jim Pancero, a brilliant sales trainer and speaker I've had the pleasure of working with, always challenges his clients to answer a question that any customer might ask: "With all of the competitive alternatives available to me, why should I buy from you?" In other words, "what is your *unique value proposition*?"

There is no single best type of product offering. Your product offering will be based upon your strategy and unique value proposition. But regardless of the type of offering you select, you must determine how your customer bundles the products. As an extreme example, a medical equipment supplier wouldn't also sell automobile tires. If you chose to operate in the medical equipment category, where the potential scope of the offering is huge to begin with, your more logical choices would be between high-end medical devices and repetitive disposables (gauze, tape, cotton, etc).

The choice depends on the second "P;" the *place* you select to sell your products.

Place Strategy

Place is a combination of the types of customers you want to serve, the market channels that access those customers and the geographic markets you want to be in. Many marketers don't spend enough time on the place strategy. Your ability to access markets is probably more of a stumbling block than you realize.

Most people assume that doing business over the Internet is the ultimate in easy *place* access. I too made this naïve assumption. After all, put up your website and anyone in the world can view it and buy directly from you. Well, while that may be technically true, getting access to your target customers isn't that easy.

I wrote and produced a CD-based seminar called "The Six Figure Job Search" to help executives with the entire job search process. I registered my domain name, www.sixfigurejobsearch.com and hired a quality web designer to set it all up. Before I knew it, I was in business – or so I thought. After the first four weeks I received a total of ZERO hits.

So, I paid for higher visibility in the major search engines. I targeted Google, Yahoo and MSN to have my website come up when people typed in certain key words. After a second four weeks, I got 100 hits and ZERO sales. So, eight weeks after opening for business on the World Wide Web, a mere 100 people tripped over my site – none of whom bought the CD.

Undeterred, I contacted a friend of mine, Michael Allen, the founder and CEO of CEOTRAK Media, Inc. CEOTRAK is an incredibly useful portal for business executives in need of everything from news to acquisition support. Michael explained to this Internet neophyte that adding links across the web also increases hit rates by moving you closer to the top of *other* search engines' search results. He also was kind enough to feature my website on CEOTRAK. From there, I asked each of the people who provided a testimonial for Six Figure Job Search if we could cross-link our sites. They all agreed.

Then I went low tech with classified advertising in newspapers in the top 10 US markets and in popular business newsletters. I also advertised as part of other companies' opt-in e-mailing lists. All of this took about five months. Now I'm receiving thousands of hits every month and orders every day.

It took just as long, and cost just as much, to get access to the market as it did to produce and publish the CD.

(Incidentally, this particular Real World Story was also an unapologetic example of cross marketing!)

I've seen my experience occur again and again in all areas of business... companies that have the product nailed, the target market nailed, the advertising nailed, but who don't fully determine how best to access the market because they assume the market will beat a path to their door.

As part of the marketing process, everyone should map the channels to market and how to access those channels. It is also essential to determine whether the channel players will welcome you or try to block you. If your marketing strategy has any impact on their status quo, even if that impact is positive, expect severe resistance from the channels to market. Most markets view any change in the status quo as a serious threat rather than an opportunity.

Real World Story No. 10

In the world of building materials used in commercial markets (offices, schools, retail, hotels, etc), most products flow first from the manufacturer to distributors, and second from the distributors to the contractors that install them. In the metal-framing market segment I work in, we were able to actually grow the overall market for this product through the development of an entirely new way to construct a building.

The system was proven, as was our profitability. Also proven were the channel and the significant cost savings in store for building owners. Yet, distributors at first were highly resistant. Why? Because it increased the manufacturers' influence with contractors. The distributors viewed this as a potential threat and loss of leverage. When we first launched this system in a region, we had to devote as much time and energy to keeping the channel from blocking our efforts as we did in promoting the system itself.

If I had kept this lesson in mind when I launched my CD, I could have ensured access to the market quicker, and for much less time and money. Hopefully you will remember it sooner than I did.

Later in this chapter we will dig into how to develop a customer strategy that significantly impacts the larger *place* strategy. But first we must make sure the remaining "Ps" are also understood.

Price Strategy

The first thing to remember about pricing your product is that *nobody buys on price alone.* You can literally and figuratively take that truism to the bank! If people bought on price alone, all of us would be driving $10,000 cars – or whatever the cheapest new car costs these days.

This truism even applies in the case of pure commodity items. If commodities were purchased on price alone, why would anyone buy milk at a convenience store? After all, supermarkets sell the same milk for a lot less.

The fact is that all purchasing decisions, whether business-to-business (B2B) or business-to-consumer (B2C), are based on the same four purchase-decision criteria:

1. Risk reduction
2. Profit improvement (savings, in the case of B2C)
3. The hassle factor
4. Ego.

Risk Reduction

Is yours a start-up company or one that is venturing into a new field? If so, it will be perceived as riskier to do business with than more established companies. The upshot of this is that potential clients will discount your product compared to the prevailing market price. On the other hand, by reducing a customer's risk of doing business, you can earn a risk-reduction premium.

Real World Story No. 11

My wife will only drive a Volvo. She had an accident more than ten years ago in a car built buy one of the Big Three that was likely due to faulty brakes. Now, this wasn't a major accident, but our youngest daughter was in the car with her, and that made my wife more conscious of safety.

The car was repairable, and the dealer was to expedite everything. But not until four months and many crappy loaner and rental cars had come and gone did we finally get the car back from the dealer. And it was clear that no care had been taken in getting it fixed.

That weekend, my wife traded the car in on a new Volvo. The dealer treated her royally and demonstrated that doing business at the dealership reduced risk through superior service and a product that was built to be safe. Ten years and three Volvos later, my wife still won't look at another car.

Profit Improvement

The building system product I talked about in an earlier Real World Story shows how customers select vendors who can improve their profits. At the very least, you have to demonstrate that your product *won't reduce* profits. Life-cycle costing, direct costs and higher margins that can be earned with your product all qualify when making this point. But it must be real and it must be quantifiable. Don't assume the customer will do the math or make the same assumptions you make; rather, you should define how the customer will view the financial aspects of the transaction.

In the context of B2C, consumers think in terms of savings. Special financing is an example of a savings motive.

The Hassle Factor

Convenience stores are called that for a reason – a reason that also explains why people will spend 25% more in a convenience store for staples like milk. The hassle factor can be huge in both B2B and B2C buying decisions.

Because saving time is valued as highly as anything else these days, companies that are quick and easy to do business with can earn a premium in their market price. For this reason, it's important to be seen as offering the path of least resistance when customers compare your company and its competitors.

Ego

Ego applies equally to B2B and luxury consumer goods. People like doing business with well-known companies. I've known many purchasing managers to enjoy dropping the names of well-known CEOs they've had lunch with. I can assure you that those purchasing managers paid a little bit more here and there for those bragging rights.

Ego factors don't have to be overly obvious symbols such as expensive cars. Egos can also be stroked by making them feel just a little more important or worthwhile. Every person responds a little differently, so feeding an ego correctly takes careful consideration.

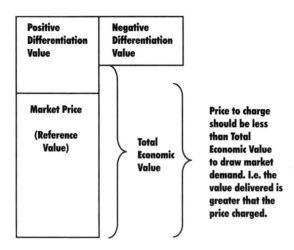

SPG's Economic Value Analysis Model

How much will these factors help your company earn or lose a premium to market? Here's a simple tool that can be utilized with the four purchasing factors. I learned of it at a seminar by the Strategic Pricing Group (www.StrategicPricingGroup.com). SPG's Economic Value Analysis Model says that every company has both positive and negative value differentiators that determine whether the price you can earn will be a premium or a discount to market – and the size of that premium or discount.

I incorporate the four purchase-decision criteria (risk reduction, profit improvement, the hassle factor and ego) into this model to develop an analysis of the positive and negative value differentials between my company and its competitors. By educating my team on the four criteria and the Economic Value Analysis Model, we all have a common way of thinking and talking about price and value. It also has provided us with a basis for making strategic decisions because it tests the competitive assumptions that our pricing tactics are based on.

The key take-away is that pricing is a much more complex process than deciding how much you charge for your product. Both quantitative and qualitative factors go into pricing strategy.

For more information on pricing strategy and analysis, I recommend "The Strategy and Tactics of Pricing" by Thomas Nagle (founder of the Strategic Pricing Group) and Reed Holden.

Promotion Strategy

Promotion is all about communicating to your target market who you are, what you do and how you do it. Think back to the questions we identified in the previous chapter: "Who are we?" "Where are we going?" and "How are we going to get there?" Promotion is nothing more than communicating the answers to these questions in a manner that captures customers' attention and makes them want to do business with you.

Companies tend to make three common mistakes in formulating their promotion strategies:

1. Playing to their own egos
2. Being too subtle
3. Overshadowing the product or service being sold.

Playing to Our Own Egos

The normal warning sign that a company has fallen into this trap is a promotional campaign based on the fact that they're the biggest, the oldest or the company with the broadest product offerings. Do those attributes bring value to the customer? Worse, do they overlook the preference many customers have for smaller, younger companies operating leaner with fresh thinking and tightly focused specialties?

Another warning sign of an ego-based promotion is one that features the CEO or owner of the business. In those rare cases where the individual has earned a reputation for expertise in the field (Lee Iacocca comes to mind) the promotion can make sound business sense. Otherwise, it's just a transparent exercise in ego-stroking.

Real World Story No. 12

The Canadian division of a company I worked for a few years back had decided that touting how great and smart its staff was would be a terrific way to promote the company to the market. So they had a photographer shoot their top executives and sales managers and had professional writers develop their bios and a success story or two for a printed piece.

They spent thousands of dollars and proudly sent the piece out to the market. It was designed to resemble a playbill in which each of the actors' roles was represented by a write-up and head shot. One of their larger Canadian customers – someone I knew from my days there – called me in hysterics when he received the brochure. Interestingly, his reaction to this obvious exercise in navel gazing was to be concerned about continuing to do business with any company that showed such bad judgment.

Promotion That Is Too Subtle

In an attempt to avoid the ego trap, some companies will promote their products in very subtle ways. You may recall AT&T's multi-million-dollar advertising during the Super Bowl a few years ago introducing M Life. The commercials that led up to the Super Bowl didn't tell you what M Life was – just that it would "change everything." Then when the big unveiling occurred, we learned that M Life was a cell-phone service from AT&T, but nothing about how it was going to change everything. Boy, I still question the decision-making process that went into that promotion.

Promotion That Overshadows What's Being Promoted

This is a classic mistake in television promotion. How many times have you seen an incredibly creative commercial that you describe the next day to your colleagues at work … but you can't remember the advertiser? Advertising agencies that overly indulge their creative people often sacrifice communication for "creativity."

Real World Story No. 13

One promotional effort I heard about was both clever and memorable. In five words, it communicated who the sponsor was, what it did and how it did it.

It was by a small barbershop facing the new challenge of a haircut chain that had moved in directly across the street with a sign reading "Home of the $7 Hair Cut!" Instead of surrendering to the competition and moving to a new location, the small proprietor capitalized on his belief that people value the quality of the haircuts they receive. So, instead of "For Sale," his sign read, "We Fix $7 Hair Cuts!"

When it comes to well-conceived promotions, it doesn't get any better than that!

A Few Thoughts on Internet Promotion

The Internet has certainly changed the world over the last ten years… probably in more ways than we even realize. I have already shared my little Internet venture with you, but I also have worked on large Internet projects as a member of the executive teams at three large publicly traded companies.

The first thing to consider when developing a website is the purpose of the site. There are only four possible purposes:

1. To sell (transact business)
2. To inform and promote
3. To work (gather data, share data, etc)
4. A combination of the above

The second order of business is to avoid falling in love with high-tech glitzy gimmicks for the site. The tech is the means, not the end. But by all means avoid the opposite pole – the amateurish "my nephew did it" look. Use a quality web designer. Third, remember that people suddenly develop attention deficit disorder the moment they access the web. Unless they are gathering highly technical mission-critical data, B2B and B2C surfers jump around the Internet the nanosecond they become bored with a site. Your site has to grab people's attention quickly, provide the information they're looking for quickly and be simple as well as intuitive to navigate.

Finally, remember that the web is no longer about simply putting up a site and the world beating a path to your door. To get a percentage of the billion or so surfers out there versus the hundreds of thousands of key word hits that your site may be listed under requires creativity and sometimes low-tech means of driving people there.

Customer Strategy

A strategic plan, supported by marketing strategy and tactics, ultimately needs to drive an actionable customer plan that delivers sales. After all, without a sale, nothing else matters. There is only one line of revenue on the P&L statement, and that is Sales.

But *revenue* and *profit* are two different things. In terms of the bottom line, selling to certain customers is more profitable than selling to others. With the increasing realization that all of a company's customers are not created equal when it comes to adding value has come an increased reliance on the process of *customer segmentation*. By segmenting its customers according to specific criteria, a company identifies the ones that can drive the most value and also be less likely to switch to a competitor for price alone.

The best customer-segmentation analyses provide quantifiable results. This is not an exercise in deciding who is more fun to do business with, or who your sales people like the most. To start this process, you first need to determine the criteria that are most important to your company.

Real World Story No. 14

I've led this process at two B2B companies. What I describe here works best in B2B companies with less than 2,000 customers. It begins with a good, old-fashioned brainstorming session to come up with a list of ten or twelve criteria that a cross-functional team can use to determine the value of a given customer.

Next, the list is circulated to a larger group for comment. If we learn the original team overlooked anything, we decide whether the list should be changed. Once the list is finalized, it must be weighted to reflect importance or impact. For example, at one company we considered our ability to gain more share with an account as the most important and weighted that highest (5 out of 5). We then set the criteria up with the weighting in an Excel spreadsheet so that as we rated customers one through five, with one being the lowest score, the worksheet automatically tabulated the scores.

Segmentation Worksheet	Increase Share			Product Mix		
Customer	Rating	Weight	Score	Rating	Weight	Score
Big Company Inc.	1	5	5	3	2	6
Acme Corporation	3	5	15	4	2	8
Joe LLC	5	5	25	3	2	6

Etc.

When all the categories are scored, the spreadsheet totals a score for each customer. The key is to rate the number of customers who currently make up 80 percent of your volume plus the top 10 customers in each market region who you are not currently doing business with, but you *should be doing business with*.

After the spreadsheet calculations were run, we divided the scores into four groups. The highest priority group had the top 20 percent of the scores. The second group in importance scored in the next 30 percent. The third was the next 40 percent and the least important group to us scored in the bottom 10 percent. We named these groups "Key Driver Accounts," "Contributor Accounts," "Maintenance Accounts" and "Reposition Accounts."

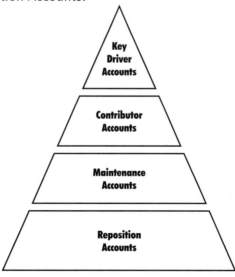

Key Driver Accounts

Contributor Accounts

Maintenance Accounts

Reposition Accounts

With our customers segmented, we evaluated how we were currently investing our assets in these accounts. What we found was that we underinvested in the Key Driver and Contributor Accounts and were highly overinvested in the Reposition Accounts, which drove the least value for us.

When I presented this to our CEO, he took a slightly jaundiced view of "firing" customers. I had to convince him that we wouldn't drop any customers before gaining more position with the Key Driver Accounts. The results? After the first year, we actually were doing business with fewer customers but had maintained our share. More exactly, we had *improved the quality of our share* through this process!

What are key-driver, contributor, maintenance and reposition accounts? Essentially, you define them based on the objectives of your business and the resources available to you. There is no formal recipe for defining these account types. Definitions are based on your overall strategy.

Note that the marketing strategy is not independent of the corporate strategy. While this may seem like a "no duh" statement, there often are real-world incongruities between a company's overall strategy and its marketing strategy. A good general manager will bring these discrepancies to the attention of management.

One More Tool

Before this chapter ends, I'd like to give you one more mental model to use – the idea of viewing the tools of marketing as a map, a compass and radar.

The map describes the market in detail and is drawn from the answers to questions used in the strategic-planning process:

- Who are the customers?
- How big is the opportunity?
- Who are the competitors?
- What is their strategy?
- How are we positioned/perceived in the market?
- What other markets could we/should we be in?

The compass shows us where to navigate within the map – a continuous 360 degree scan of the market landscape. It is guided by the 4 "Ps:"

- Product
- Place
- Price
- Promotion

The radar identifies sudden changes in competition or market landscape.

- Assessment of competitive reactions to our moves
- Identification of new market opportunities
- Analysis of the market, end user and channel customer trends

To wrap up this chapter, it is worth quoting Yogi Berra again, "If you don't know where you are going, you might not ever get there." By thinking and acting like a general manager, you will know the map of your company's marketing plan, you will know the direction and destination your company is heading toward and you will be sensitive to blips on the company's market radar.

Chapter 5:
Crisis Management

In This Chapter:

- Emotional Control
- Well-Established Procedures
- Good Communication
- Focus on Working the Problem
- Transfer the Experience

Although the word "crisis" in the business setting includes extremely dire situations like anthrax-laced letters and product failures that cause serious injury or death, most of the crises a manager must deal with are much less dramatic. Nevertheless, they can be very disruptive to productivity and can have significant impact on the company.

The typical crisis confronting a general manager involves angry customers, the unexpected departure of key employees, product-quality issues, sudden and unforeseen changes in the market or an attack by a competitor.

Your ability to respond effectively to a crisis requires solid teamwork from the staff you have developed and the strength of the relationships you have built with other functions in the organization. You will soon learn how effective you have been in these areas, and how well you have progressed as a general manager.

The first thing to remember is that not all crises can be foreseen or avoided. Shit happens. But you still must know how to recognize a potential crisis before it boils over, how to react to it and who to trust for reliable information. Rushing into full CYA mode (covering your ass) is *not* managing a crisis.

To learn how best to deal with a crisis, it is instructive to look at professionals who operate in crisis mode most of the time, such as emergency medical technicians and firemen. What qualities generally characterize these people?

1. Emotional control
2. Adherence to well-established procedures
3. Good communication
4. Strong focus on working the problem
5. Transferring experience from one event to the next

Emotional Control

Maintaining emotional control is key to dealing with a crisis. Imagine your reaction if the fireman called to release you from a wrecked car appeared to be panicking – or the EMTs transporting you to the hospital. You expect them to operate with a sense of urgency, but that isn't the same as a panic reaction.

Your ability to avoid overreacting in the face of a crisis – the most common mistake in crisis management – will be improved if you realize that crises can happen regardless of how capable you or your team are. Overreacting will only make matters worse and create the perception that the crisis is worse than it is. Panic is overreaction on steroids.

While speed to solution is one of the critical elements of dealing with a crisis, it's essential to curb the instinct to run off in several directions at once without a plan. As Colin Powell said, "Nothing is a good as or as bad as originally reported." That's why gathering reliable facts must be standard operating procedure in crisis management.

At the opposite pole is the "head in the sand" approach. Some managers simply don't act at all, hoping the situation will correct itself. Unfortunately, a crisis is not like wine; it doesn't improve with age. A crisis is more like fish; the longer it sits, the worse it smells.

I've found myself with at least one Chicken Little on my staff at every company I've worked for. It's taught me to be cautious when dealing with them, because there's usually a kernel of truth behind their assertions that the sky is falling! (And at least they raise problems rather than sweeping them under the rug.) As tempting as it can be to ignore their ravings, there also is a risk of overlooking a brewing crisis and engendering even broader panic when it surfaces.

In cases where there was some substance to their concerns, I've found it important to meet with the Chicken Littles after the storm passes, to point out where their actions were correct and helpful and where they were not. I like to ask them if they feel their response was measured and appropriate, and how they would handle the situation the next time. In time, Chicken Little is replaced by a more effective employee.

While you're at it, you should also ask *yourself* if you or your organization breed the Chicken Little reaction through a tradition of head-in-the-sand reactions to potential crises. Is making a federal case out of any issue the only way your employees can be certain of being heard?

The third major mistake many managers make is to react to a crisis by launching an immediate witch hunt. This is the most damaging reaction of all, because not only will it not solve the problem, it triggers the CYA mentality that kills communication up and down the chain and across functions.

Well-Established Procedures

The first thing emergency workers do in a crisis is to conduct a rapid assessment of the facts. Having done that, they're ready to implement procedures established in response to handling many similar past situations.

In business, production facilities and functions such as trucking and shipping require well-documented and well-communicated procedures to ensure that safety, environmental and quality concerns are effectively addressed.

The lack of well-established or well-communicated procedures can lead to incidents like the accidental spilling of 10 million gallons of oil into Alaska's Prince William Sound by the tanker Exxon Valdez. Although it was a procedural violation that first caused the ship to run aground, it was Exxon's failure to deploy booms to contain the spill in less than 10 hours that resulted in widespread environmental devastation. After first saying that state and local agencies had delayed the containment process, Exxon later admitted it delayed because it wasn't sure of the procedures for containing spills in the Sound.

Having well documented and well communicated procedures and "dry run" drills to master them can keep a small problem from mushrooming into a major disaster.

This lesson isn't limited to production facilities, trucking and shipping. It applies to all areas of a business. What should the sales organization do with a customer complaint? What should accounts receivable do when a major account files for bankruptcy? What should human resources do if there is sudden turnover or an accusation of wrongdoing or harassment?

Each requires that proper procedures be developed.

Good Communication

When the EMTs wheel you into the hospital, they immediately pass on the facts they have collected to the Emergency Room doctor. In fact, they also relay information originally gathered by the firemen and police who were first on the scene, which also may include information from witnesses. In this example, no one has any reason to withhold information.

In business and politics, a CYA mindset inhibits the flow of good communication about a problem. Remember what I said at the beginning of this chapter: crisis situations are the acid test of your general management skills, and the quality and speed of communications are your key performance indicators.

Let's say you suddenly lost a top key driver account that will impact your top line and bottom line. Where do you go for the information you need? The answer is *as close to the source of the problem as possible*, while still respecting the chain of command by sharing everything you learned within the chain.

This also is known as "verifying the verifier." By directly going to the original source, you can locate any inconsistencies in the communications. But you also must pass the information back along the chain of command or risk fostering distrust. If you find that information was filtered, you can address it after the crisis is resolved. Remember: work the problem *first* and deal with causes when the crisis passes.

Make sure you gather information from a variety of perspectives. If the customer claimed that quality was one of the main reasons for their departure, go directly to the production people. You may find that quality was not the problem, but only an excuse covering up the real reason the customer left. On the other hand, you may find the sales people approved shipping substandard product as the result of scheduling concerns. Or hundreds of different pieces of information.

By listening to all sides, you gather all the pieces of the puzzle.

An example of this is a procedure requiring plant managers to report lost-time accidents to the divisional president. This accomplishes two things. First, the president hears firsthand about the accident and can determine the potential severity of the situation to the employee and the company. If the situation is grim, he or she can assign key VPs to manage it. Second, it calls attention to the importance and priority of factory safety. Because no plant manager wants to have to call the president to report a lost-time accident, he or she will be highly focused on implementing and communicating necessary policies and procedures to ensure a safe working environment.

Focus on Working the Problem

We've covered most of this topic already, but it bears some repeating because it is so easy to become distracted from working the problem *first*.

If you were on a gurney in an Emergency Room and the doctor kept asking what caused the accident rather than determining the nature of your injuries, the odds of your recovery would get much longer. The odds of recovering a key driver account would also worsen if you spent all your time trying to assign blame.

The answer is to work the problem and ignore the momentary emotions and issues that are peripheral to problem solving.

Transfer the Experience

How did the Emergency Room doctor know what to do when you were brought into the hospital? Well, the knowledge she or he learned from treating hundreds of car-accident victims provided clues as to what to look for.

Airbags are standard equipment in cars today, and have saved countless thousands of lives. But before the technology was well developed, the violent force of airbag deployment actually resulted in fatal injuries in a number of cases. Through their experience, Emergency Room doctors were able to provide manufacturers with information that helped make airbags safer and extremely effective.

Once you have worked the situation and your business crisis is in the rearview mirror, the time is at hand to determine how it developed into a crisis, accountability for it, and to consider procedures that can prevent avoidable crises from reoccurring. By this time, emotions and the CYA reflex should no longer inhibit cool logic.

Henry Ford said, "Failure is only the opportunity to begin again more intelligently." The same holds true for managing a crisis better the second time.

Beginning again more intelligently begins with asking the following questions:

1. Should we have been able to see this crisis coming?
   a. If so, why didn't we see it?
   b. Who should be responsible for monitoring and communicating this type of issue?
   c. What policies or procedures need to be updated or changed as a result?
2. If it was impossible to see this crisis coming, was our reaction to it appropriate?
   a. If not, what should we have done?
   b. Do we need to develop policies or procedures for dealing with this type of crisis in the future?

Real World Story No. 15

Following the attacks of September 11, 2001, American intelligence services were criticized for giving insufficient attention to the increased "chatter" among suspected terrorists, and for their failure to share the information with other government agencies. One of the reasons for the creation of the Department of Homeland Security was to prevent a repetition of the problem.

At my company, we have a very detailed call report system that gathers as many facts as possible about the customer. The system was developed in response to learning that we could have averted past customer crises by listening to the chatter that surfaces in routine conversations and communicating it effectively throughout the organization.

The call report system incorporates four different alert buttons. One, for instance, is a credit alert button that would be pressed by a sales person who learned that a customer was beginning to get into financial trouble. In response to such an alert, the credit department would investigate the situation.

The second thing we did was train our organization to take call reports seriously, and not just as another administrative task to be dispensed with as quickly as possible. We also conducted training on writing call reports that increased consistency and made calls more comparable.

Third, we made sure every call report is read. Given that thousands of sales calls are made every month, this is no small task. In addition to myself, hundreds of reports are read monthly by our regional managers, director of customer relations and even the president. By exchanging notes on specific calls as warranted, we have been able to distill the "chatter" and assemble the information into an intelligible whole.

For example, let's say that a large national customer in a given territory starts to reduce its purchases from us. The local sales rep investigates and concludes from the information received that it is a local issue requiring that he or she build a better relationship with the local purchasing manager. This might be the beginning and the end of it, but what if the local rep missed some of the chatter and the same thing is happening in other sales territories? By paying attention to all of the information we gather, we would be much more likely to uncover a customer's strategy to give a little of our share to one of our competitors. Even if the customer is trying to keep their plan below our radar, we should be able to detect and deal with it before the real damage can be done by assembling all the puzzle pieces.

George Santayana wrote, "Those who ignore history are doomed to repeat it." I'll close this chapter by quoting George Bernard Shaw, who remarked of Santayana's quote, "If history repeats itself, and the unexpected always happens, how incapable must Man be of learning from experience."

We will always be capable of anticipating the unexpected by simply taking the time to look back and learn.

People Skills

The Lost Art of General Management

Chapter 6:
The Leadership Imperative

In This Chapter:

- What *Is* Leadership, Anyway?
- The Seven Key Indicators of Leadership
  - Emotional Intelligence
  - Ability to Articulate the Mission, Vision and Strategy
  - Integrity and Trust
  - Caring for the Organization and Its People
  - The Ability to Roll with the Punches
  - The Ability to Nurture Strong Followers
  - Delivering Results Over the Long Haul
- Common Misconceptions About Leadership
  - Viewing Leadership as Just Another Skill
  - The Fallacy of Believing There's Only One "Right" Leadership Style
  - The Fallacy of Believing Leaders Are Born, Not Made

A great deal already has been written on the topic of leadership, and surely a lot more will follow. My objective in writing on this subject is not just to add to the volumes that already exist – it is to specifically explain why leadership is the single most important dimension affecting any organization. That's why this chapter is titled "The Leadership Imperative."

A company can have the best mission, vision, and strategy in its industry, but without leadership it is destined to drift off course and onto the rocks. Conversely, good leadership can overcome an average mission, vision and strategy because outstanding execution of even an average strategy can often lead to success.

Leadership is one of those things that everyone realizes is necessary but is hard pressed to define. And it's very hard to foresee in job candidates.

Leadership and management are not the same thing, even though the two often are confused. John P. Kotter, a frequent contributor to the *Harvard Business Review*, explains this in the context of the military:

"A peacetime army can usually survive with good administration and management up and down the hierarchy, coupled with good leadership concentrated at the very top. A wartime army, however, needs competent leadership at all levels. No one yet has figured out how to manage people effectively into battle; they must be led into battle."

What *Is* Leadership, Anyway?

Leadership is a tangible quality. When you're in the presence of a strong leader, you know it.

That's not to say, however, that leadership is easy to define. I think the best way to explain the elusive commodity we think of as leadership is to list the qualities and behaviors that effective leaders display.

The Seven Key Indicators of Leadership

I believe the key indicators of leadership are:

1. Emotional intelligence
2. The ability to communicate a company's mission, vision and strategy clearly to anyone in the organization
3. Integrity and trust
4. Caring for the organization and the people
5. An ability to roll with the punches and deal effectively with the inevitable trials and tribulations
6. An ability to nurture capable followers
7. Delivering results, especially over the long haul

You may be asking, "what about charisma?" Well, it's fair to say that anyone who demonstrates the seven indicators of leadership must have charisma. But it's also important to avoid confusing "larger than life" personalities with charismatic ones.

In the previous chapter, I explained the importance of the ability to communicate the mission, vision and strategy clearly to everyone in the organization. Here's my take on the remaining indicators:

Emotional Intelligence

Great leaders seem to have a sixth sense about how people and groups feel and how they will react to different stimuli. These leaders are said to have high "emotional intelligence."

Emotional intelligence was brought to the forefront in Daniel Goleman's book of the same name. His concept has influenced many psychologists in the understanding of emotional development and its effects on personal success. Emotional intelligence is defined as the ability to manage our emotional mind with intelligence in every facet of life. Our reactions to situations and people are the result of our unique and individual combination of thinking and feeling. Our specific manner of comprehending situations dictates our subsequent reactions.

Aristotle put it best more than two millennia ago; "Anyone can become angry – that is easy. But to be angry with the right person, to the right degree, at the right time, for the right purpose, and the right way – this is not easy."

While we are all born with a certain combination of emotional intelligence and intellectual intelligence, education teaches that we can grow our intellect. Therefore, the same applies to our emotional intellect. It needs the same fostering, nurturing and development.

This is a very complicated subject. In addition to reading the Goleman book, I recommend contacting the Center for Creative Leadership at www.ccl.com. CCL's premise is that learning more about your own personality and leadership style will enable you to better understand the impact you have on others and become a more effective leader. This is not a cookie-cutter approach. I also recommend *Harvard Business Review on Leadership*, a compilation of the publication's best articles on leadership as selected by its editors.

Integrity and Trust

The accounting scandals of 2001 and 2002 have made the importance of integrity and trust obvious through the unfortunate fact that those qualities have gone missing in even some of the nation's most respected firms.

I would argue that a person who loses his or her integrity cannot be considered to possess any personal assets. If people don't trust you, how can you lead? You may be able to use fear and power to get short-term results, but you won't get results over the long term. At some point, the troops will rebel.

Real World Story No. 16

One of the greatest compliments I ever received in business was from a large and important customer who was introducing me to the president of a firm in which he had a large ownership stake. The firm happened to be a good potential customer for us.

When he realized that the president wasn't sure if relying on my company would be good for his business, my customer said of me, "This guy is true blue. I don't always like what he has to say, but he is the most honest guy I know in this industry. His word you can take to the bank."

That endorsement alone got us the business with the prospect. The commodity industry I was in wasn't necessarily known for its straightforwardness and honesty. We decided that integrity and honesty would be our key differentiator. A customer satisfaction survey we had conducted told us we were considered the most trusted company in the industry, with the most trusted sales organization.

Trust and integrity will carry you over any of the rough patches with a customer, peer, boss or employee.

Caring for the Organization and Its People

This is related to trust and integrity. If you really don't care about the people you work with, you won't be able to deliver long-term results. Treating the people you work with as though they were merely tools for getting the job done isn't leadership. It's essential to recognize that every employee has ambitions, needs and fears just as you do. They're also looking to you for help in achieving satisfaction from their work.

Unfortunately, many managers believe that demonstrating care for their people relieves them of the accountability for delivering the results they're responsible for. Leadership and compassion are not mutually exclusive.

Managers also must show that they sincerely care for their companies. If you are perceived as just being in it for the income or to meet your personal agenda, not only will it be hard to get your people to follow, it also will be hard to get the support of your superiors. If you can't buy in to who your company is, where it is going and how it is going to get there, *what are you doing there?*

The Ability to Roll With the Punches

Shit happens. It's inevitable that something will go wrong on your watch.

When the world doesn't go according to how you think it should, it's important to show grace under pressure. A leader who panics doesn't instill confidence in the troops. If you're panicking, they wonder if they should be, too. If you react by lashing out with anger, how can they be expected to rise to the challenge and solve the crisis? They're much more likely to keep their heads down, holing up in their offices hoping that you won't see them.

Calm evaluation of any problems is in order. Managers need to get the facts and manage by the facts. This creates an atmosphere that inspires employees to come directly to you as soon as they see a problem occurring. If this atmosphere is missing, you won't find out until the problem is much worse and more difficult to solve.

Colin Powell said, "Nothing is as good as or as bad as originally reported." I agree completely, which means the most appropriate response to bad news is always to react calmly and to keep a level head – at least until you can get a full assessment of the situation!

One of the standards I set for myself is that I didn't want my boss to ever be surprised by information that I should have conveyed or should have known but didn't. This is a hard standard to achieve, but an important one to work by.

The eight bosses I've had over the last 20 years have demonstrated the full spectrum of responses to trials and tribulations. I can assure you that the bosses that showed grace under pressure were best able to lead their teams and rise to the challenge. I had one boss in particular who typically overreacted, shot the messenger and spent more time on assigning blame and "spinning" the problem instead of devoting his energies to the problem itself. While personal pride kept most of us going, many members of the team slipped into an apathetic coma. The situation actually led to my looking to work for another company.

In gauging your reactions to situations, think about what kind of reaction you would expect a great leader to have. Think about specific leaders who have motivated you over the years and how they would have reacted. This is a good self-monitoring system to help you ensure that your reactions to situations will strengthen your leadership position, rather than hinder it.

An Ability to Nurture Capable Followers

Before a person becomes a leader he or she is a follower. In fact, everyone with the exception of a dictator *remains a follower* throughout their careers because there's always someone higher to report to.

Our military academies have graduated innumerable great leaders. But every one of them began as a plebe in a system that teaches overconfident freshmen to check their egos at the door and take orders for the good of the unit. In other words, the freshman are taught how to be followers first and leaders second. "Followership" is the foundation of a military education, according to Army Colonel Larry Donnithorne, author of *The West Point Way of Leadership.*

Liz Ryan of Liz Ryan Consulting has assembled a list called "Ten Things Your Manager Wants You to Know." I've found it very useful for assuring myself that I'm adding value to my relationship with my boss. Liz' list is reprinted here:

1. Don't take it personally when I'm abrupt. Bosses don't necessarily handle stress any better than you.

2. I can't make a federal case out of every issue that's important to you. When it comes to doing battle with my own boss or other departments, please let me pick my battles on your behalf.

3. I am not King Solomon. When you and a co-worker both want the desk next to the window, play rock-paper-scissors.
4. Don't give me a reason to watch you like a hawk.
5. You're the expert on how to do your job, not me. Don't be frustrated that I don't know the intimate details. I have a different job description than you.
6. When you're angry with me let me know.
7. Don't ask me to tell you what I can't talk about, such as if layoffs are coming. I like you, but not enough to jeopardize my job.
8. Discuss with me problems as far in advance as possible. I can help you out of a jam if I have the lead time.
9. Give me feedback on my management style but be tactful and constructive.
10. I can help you if you goof up, but don't do anything really stupid.

Leaders are only as good as their followers. By demonstrating how to be a good follower to your boss, your subordinates will have a role model to emulate in their dealings with you.

Delivering Results Over the Long Haul

The ultimate mark of a great leader is the ability to deliver results consistently for long periods. While it's quite possible for most people to achieve short-term results with bad leadership skills, it takes a true leader to get results over the long haul.

Over the long term, leaders must cope with both internal and external challenges. The direction they take and how they navigate and modify their course of action will impact results over the long haul. Decisions made in early years of a leadership position will haunt or help in later years.

Common Misconceptions About Leadership

Companies that don't "get" leadership seem to go wrong in one of three areas – sometimes in all three!

These areas are:

1. Viewing leadership as just another skill, like accounting or marketing

2. Believing there is one *right* leadership style
3. Believing leaders are born and not made – the old "you've either got it or you don't" mentality.

Viewing Leadership as Just Another Skill

Leadership is what enables a general manager to be effective in his or her work. It's how he or she operates and interacts with subordinates, peers and the boss. The general manager's leadership abilities will affect everything those other people do.

How many times have you seen a highly skilled person promoted to running a department and then fail? Too often, I'll bet. Chances are, failure wasn't due to the lack of technical competence, but rather to the lack of an ability *to lead!*

How well a manager is able to employ his or her functional skills is dependent on his or her ability to lead. Too often, managers either ignore dealing with people in managing things or they simply *tell* people what to do. This is not leadership.

The problem in this approach is that the team will stop thinking for itself. This eliminates valuable opportunities for improvement that should come from the people who are closest to the work. Worse, they can easily become apathetic and stop caring about performing their jobs well. This comes from the realization that there's no reward for thinking – only for doing.

Managers who rely on the "Attila the Hun with a toothache" approach to leadership when things get rough are even more certain to kill effective communications with team members.

The Fallacy of Believing There Is Only One "Right" Leadership Style

From football coaches to US presidents, Americans have experienced a wide spectrum of effective leadership styles. So, why is it that many companies try to adopt just one style of leadership?

One possibility is they're confusing the act of building a company culture with leadership. The culture consists of common beliefs, mores and codes of conduct, so it is appropriate for all employees. Companies with this mindset often spend large sums sending their managers to various leadership seminars that promise big results if their "one size fits all" techniques are employed.

The belief in a "cookie cutter" leadership style is naïve at best, and more likely destructive, since most managers simply won't use it.

The fact is that each team, department or region is unique because every person is unique. Therefore, the effective leader must adopt a leadership style that accepts the eclectic nature of the people he or she must lead. Some groups or individuals require more of a push or a firmer hand, while others need supportive encouragement and recognition. A good leader develops a "feel" for each person and team, then coaches and leads accordingly.

Real World Story No. 17

I witnessed a unique case study at one of the Fortune 500 companies I worked for that emphasized the difference good leadership can make.

A group of five vice presidents responsible for the division were all highly capable and highly ambitious. They vied with each other for power in hopes of becoming the divisional president. The potential for negative politics was huge, and was compounded by their reporting to two different divisional presidents within a span of four years. Under the first president, the group achieved a significant amount of success in terms of profitability and employee satisfaction.

The vice presidents all respected the first president greatly. They bought into his vision and took personal accountability for delivering results. The president understood the unique emotional and motivational characteristics of each of the vice presidents and understood how to take advantage of this knowledge to drive his team forward while minimizing the politics among the members.

The second president was appointed upon his retirement. None of the five vice presidents was selected as his successor, but none felt particularly slighted. They had time, and they knew that another chance would likely come with the next rotation.

The new president had an impeccable pedigree – top name schools, Big Three consulting experience, international assignments and an impressive resume of Global 500 companies to his credit. The whole team felt there was potential to go even further by learning new skills under the new president.

However, the new president was surprisingly oblivious to the potential for politicking among the vice presidents. So, rather than get off to a fast start, the productivity of his VPs dropped. As profits and employee satisfaction began to diminish, the president began listening to whispers from individual VPs about "problems" they were having with each other.

Having bought into the politicking, the president reshuffled responsibilities and gave certain VPs more power while taking it away from others. This resulted in the politics going nuclear, rather than subsiding.

With profits further dropping and employee morale waning, doubts began to grow as to whether this president could get the job done. His answer to this was to bring in two additional VPs. The VPs he hired were quickly thrown into the political fire and operated accordingly.

You can guess the results. A further decline in profitability and the lack of employee satisfaction led a wave of high-potential up-and-coming managers to leave the company and seek less dysfunctional professional families in which to build their careers.

While this real world story is somewhat anecdotal, it's very interesting to think that two different leaders with the same exact team could produce such differing results. While there were likely other mitigating circumstances, the most significant difference was *leadership*.

The Fallacy of Believing Leaders Are Born, Not Made

The "leaders are born not made" theory ignores the fact that we are more a product of our environment than of our genetics.

We act as we are taught or as we observe. Winston Churchill's famous quote, "A lie spreads around the world before the truth gets its pants on," also applies to bad leadership practices. Bad practices tend to spread faster than good ones can arrest them.

The problem is that no one really is taught how to be a leader. Corporate America is big on teaching "gimmicky" ways of being leaders, but real leadership stems from a true understanding of what makes people tick.

Chapter 7:
Nowhere to Run, Nowhere to Hide
(Making Effective Presentations)

In This Chapter:
- Why Presentations Matter
- The 10 Elements of a Great Presentation
- The Three Types of Presentations

Why Presentations Matter

Presentations matter because leadership matters, ideas matter and communication matters. And because motivation and direction matter.

The most critical job for the general manager, when you boil it all down, is *communication*. The general manager has to be effective in communicating one-on-one, in groups and in writing. While weakness in any of these three disciplines will compromise the ability to lead, the weakness most often seen in managers is group communication. It's also the most conspicuous.

Group communication can be one of a general manager's most powerful assets. When presenting to a group, he or she has its full attention – at least at the start. The trick is to keep it.

Rather than dreading or being reticent about it, general managers should seek out opportunities to present to anyone in the company. The best way to develop any skill is through repetition. This particular skill also helps to increase personal and professional exposure.

Unfortunately, corporate presentations and sales presentations are usually either:

1. Mildly competent, or
2. Career killers

The advent of new media and technology that facilitate communication and improve our ability to convey our ideas also can have the opposite effect. If a manager has a propensity to dig a hole for himself or herself in a presentation, PowerPoint can be an earthmover on steroids that will bury the presenter totally.

On the other hand, managers who are adept at presenting and public speaking can communicate even more effectively and convincingly with these tools.

Real World Story No. 18

We've all endured them ... PowerPoint presentations that drone on forever. I call this "Death by PowerPoint."

One of my near-death-by-PowerPoint experiences occurred in Newfoundland, Canada. A company that I used to work for had a small factory there. I had flown there with the company president, a few fellow officers and Bill Drellow, the freelance writer I more recently tapped to edit this book.

After touring the plant with the staff and making the general niceties with the production folks, we settled in the conference room for the homestretch ... the PowerPoint presentation.

The projector warmed up, the presenter clicked on his computer, and I saw something that almost killed me on the spot – the little box in the lower left corner of the frame that read, "Slide 1 of 101". That's right, 101 slides!

I didn't have the heart to pull the plug on their presentation and ask them to get to the point in 20 slides or less. The team had worked very hard to improve that factory, and they deserved the chance to relate the pride of their accomplishments on their own terms. So there I sat, contemplating forms of suicide (remember *Airplane, the Movie?*) to end the pain of nonstop listening.

The moral of this story is that all we walked away from this presentation with was the impression that they worked hard and *that they presented 101 slides!* Beyond that, I couldn't have recalled three things they had tried to communicate to us 15 minutes later.

The 10 Elements of a Great Presentation

1. Before you do anything else, identify the three key points you want the audience to remember. (No more than three.)

2. Determine *why* your audience should remember these points, so you can communicate that, too.

3. Open your presentation with the "why" in such a way

that it takes no more than one minute to explain. If you can't explain to the audience why your presentation is important to them within one minute, you've lost them.

4. Never forget that the audience cares less about what you have to say than you do.

5. Remember what you learned in Fourth Grade: Speak at an appropriate rate. Not too slow or too fast. And project your voice.

6. Communicate broadly through body language as well as spoken language.

7. Don't use the podium unless you're stuck reading a speech and it's the only source of light. It's easy to create the impression you're holding on to it for dear life. Speakers who walk around a podium instead of rigidly standing behind it show more confidence, differentiate themselves from other presenters, and are more interesting to watch. Walking, talking and gesturing at the same time also is a great way to hide the yips because all the adrenaline doesn't go to the throat.

8. Be so well-rehearsed that you don't sound rehearsed. There's no substitute for preparation.

9. Review your presentation with a trusted colleague or two to ensure it says what you think it says and is easily understood.

10. When using slides –

    • Organize your presentation so the titles of the slides alone tell the story. Any other text should simply support the title.

    • Don't overuse distracting gimmicks like animation.

    • Never read the slides word for word. Their only purpose is to reinforce what the audience is hearing.

    • Never spend more than two minutes on a slide.

    • Finally, and most importantly, prepare your presentation so that you don't actually need any slides. If you can be effective without slides, you're a great presenter. If you can do that, you can use slides to enhance your presentation, rather than leaning on them like a crutch.

My editor goes even further than I do when it comes to relying on slides. An experienced speechwriter, he feels that slides should only be used when they contain the faces of alleged perps and the audience is morning roll call in the squad room!

Real World Story No. 19

Actually, Bill reminded me of one of my more effective presentations; one that I had totally forgotten about. I guess I forgot it because it came the morning after our near-death by PowerPoint experience in Newfoundland, when my mind was still numb from the 101-slide onslaught.

That morning, it was management's turn to present to the staff at the plant. My topic was the need to achieve consistent product quality – a chronic problem in those days at that particular operation. Instead of using slides with charts or graphs depicting customer satisfaction to illustrate my point, I just carried my cup of Tim Horton's coffee to the front of the room. Tim Horton's is the largest coffee and donut chain in Canada.

I told the staff that I really liked Tim Horton's coffee. I explained that any time I was anywhere in Canada, I would swing by and pick up a cup of Tim's because I knew exactly the experience I would have. It was a no-brainer; the simplest type of buying decision. However, had my experience with one or more stores become less predictable ... from world-class to third world ... I would likely try other local coffee shops or any other convenient spot.

If that happened often enough, Tim's would fix their quality problems in a hurry. But, I asked the group, what would Tim's have to do to get me back as a customer? Well, they would probably have to advertise and offer discounts (which is to say, cut price and increase costs) to get me to try their coffee again.

If I were to try Tim's coffee again, I asked them what standard they thought I would hold it to. A lower standard than my current positive experience, or higher than that? The logical answer is, a higher standard. Then, if I kept going back with higher expectations, how long would it take for my skepticism to wear off? Even if there were no further disappointments, it would be a long time. After all that, all it would take to keep me from ever going back again – regardless of the price – would be another problem.

While my "coffee speech" didn't exactly break new ground, it did drive the point home with the factory personnel about how precarious their position in the market was at the time. It helped them understand the dangers of releasing product for sale that wasn't of sufficient quality. It made it easier to see their roles through the eyes of their customers.

Because Bill remembered my talk three years later, I called the general manager of the Canadian company, which I had since left, and asked him if he remembered it. Not only did he remember it, he said people still referred to it when the subject of quality was discussed.

Lesson learned... drink more coffee during presentations and use fewer (if any) slides!

The Three Types of Presentations

There are three basic types of internal presentations that managers should be adept at delivering. There are numerous hybrids, but the three basic internal presentations are:

1. The Vision, Mission, Goal Presentation
2. The Results Presentation
3. The Change-Initiative Presentation

The general theme that can always be used and tailored to suit any of these types of presentations follows this pattern: "Who we are, where we are going and how we are going to get there."

There also are three general types of external presentations:

1. Customer Presentations
2. Supplier Presentations
3. Investor/Banker Presentations

The purpose of external presentations usually is to influence the outcome of a negotiation. Thematic elements include "What's in it for you" and "How we can do this together."

Again, presentations should always start with "Why this is important to you (the audience)".

I can't emphasize enough that if you want to succeed as a leader, you must master the art of group presentation. If you just aren't comfortable with it, there is only one way to cure your discomfort... make as many presentations as possible! Comfort and an air of controlled self-confidence will only come from experience. The more you avoid developing your presentation skills, the heavier this anchor will become on your career.

Take a course, join Toastmasters, buy a video/CD on the subject. Videotape yourself rehearsing your presentations in the comfort of your home. Start with easy small group presentations and continue to work your way up until you are comfortable regardless of how many people are in the room.

Early in my career, I was like everyone else and very nervous before making presentation. But to my credit, I guess, I never avoided them. I took a lesson from a boss who was very comfortable at doing presentations. He said, "relish it and enjoy it, because if you are good at speaking you will set yourself apart from everyone else."

He was right. I still seek every opportunity to present to a group and I actually look forward to getting fired-up before my presentations. It is a learned skill, but it's a skill that's easy to perfect through practice.

In my current position, I require all my direct reports to take a course in public speaking. The ones who jumped to the task without delay have shown amazing progress… not just in their speaking skills, but in their leadership. Why? Because the skills I have outlined become part of their general way of thinking, talking one-on-one and writing. Soon, they all become significantly stronger communicators who incorporate "why this is important to you" into their communications.

Chapter 8:
The Four Conditions of Employment

In This Chapter:

• Trust, Commitment, Caring and Buy-In

In July 2002 I had the pleasure of meeting the legendary football coach, Lou Holtz. Aside from being one of the most successful college coaches of any generation, Lou also is widely known as a great all-around human being.

I suppose most people in my situation would have asked him which games were the most memorable to him, or who his favorite players were. Instead, I asked Lou to share his secret for motivating individuals to work together in support of a team's goals. Without pausing for an instant, he said, "That's easy; it comes down to three things – trust, commitment to excellence, and caring about the team."

He went on to explain that it all starts with trust. Do I trust you and do you trust me? He defined trust as simply doing what you say you're going to do and treating people with respect. The second key, commitment to excellence, he defined as never accepting mediocrity from yourself or your teammates. And the third key was caring deeply about the team, both collectively and individually.

It was timely advice because I had been philosophizing about what I perceived as a shift in the psychological contract between employee and employer. By "psychological contract," I'm referring to what each party perceives its obligation to the other to be. Not too many years ago, the terms of the psychological contract were as simple as loyalty = employment. The employer felt an obligation to retain loyal employees and loyal employees had an expectation of continued employment. Companies such as IBM, US Steel, Armstrong World Industries, and Chrysler embraced this "cradle to grave" concept.

But everyone knows that has changed. In the case of IBM, it was the coming of Microsoft and the Internet combined with some tough business cycles that rocked their commitment to the concept. For US Steel, it was foreign competition. Armstrong was racked by lawsuits involving the presence of asbestos. And is Chrysler even an American company anymore, or is it a German Company? Many Chrysler vehicles are assembled in Mexico with engines built in Canada – while their stock is traded in Germany on the DAX exchange.

In every case, external factors forced a change in the psychological contract. With the accelerating pace of change in companies and with employees less and less likely to stay for a long time (becoming less "loyal," if you will), how should the concept of the psychological contract affect the conditions of employment – yours and the people you're responsible for?

What follows is my take on the Gospel according to Lou Holtz.

Trust, Commitment, Caring and Buy-In

Trust: Do you trust the company and does the company trust you? Do you do what you say you're going to do? Do you treat the people you work with respectfully? How does the company treat you in this regard?

Commitment to Excellence: Should you get a raise every year if you're only doing enough to get by? Should all your direct reports get similar yearly increases if they're not contributing equally? Regardless of what Woody Allen said, 80 percent of life isn't "just showing up." As a general manager, you're entitled to expect the best effort from each of your team members – just as it's expected of you.

This involves candid self assessment, so you should continually ask yourself, "What can I do better? Where do I need more training? Am I really giving it my all?" And ask your direct reports the same questions!

Caring About the Team: Do you care about the company, its people and its customers? Do your direct reports care? To paraphrase President Kennedy, your inclination shouldn't be to ask "What can my company do for me?" but rather, "What can I do for my company, my direct reports, my boss and my peers?"

Buying Into the Strategy. This fourth principal comes from my personal experience, and it requires you to buy into the company's strategy. This is critical, and time and again I've seen what happens when it isn't followed.

This situation usually arises with managers who have many years of service at companies undergoing a paradigm shift. With the world changing around them, they cling to the way things used to be as though they were hanging on to a lifeboat in the North Atlantic. Anyone who's read "Who Moved

My Cheese?" knows that the characters of Hem and Haw illustrate the point I'm making here.

One of the companies I worked for was able to grow its market share substantially through a major acquisition. The acquired company also provided entree into new lines of business and new markets. Consequently, we had to change our strategy to make this acquisition a success. The upshot was tremendous change, both for us and the acquisition.

Can you guess how the majority of the people acted following the acquisition? They hunkered down and clung to the way things had been. Only a minority of managers seemed to greet change with an open mind, and even fewer viewed their role as that of a catalyst for positive change.

Because we knew there would be a "big bang," the president and I went on the road to each of the company's locations to explain the strategy behind the move and the rationale for change. Part of our message was that we all would be working for a new, more exciting company with greater opportunities for career development.

Despite the time and energy every member of the management team devoted to communicating these messages, there was still a tremendous number of people who simply couldn't let go of the past. We had no choice but to force them to support the new strategy as a condition of employment. This effectively put many of them on notice, and many others left of their own accord. We also brought in many new people from outside the company to help speed the change, not in just strategy, but also in culture.

How did things work out for us? Well, although most major acquisitions aren't successful, this one was. As a matter of fact, the integration process was completed ahead of schedule. The organization settled down and began to drive the implementation of the new strategy.

Despite our success, I can't help but think about the talent that was lost and the waste that was created because a number of valuable managers couldn't deal with having their cheese moved. Some became outright subversive and we had no choice but to release them. Some totally ignored the new opportunities they had been given and became bitter at having to accept change. And others acted like deer in the headlights. The sad thing is that none of these folks had to put themselves through that trauma.

Accurately gauging the degree to which employees buy into a company's strategy is very difficult for a general manager. Becoming sensitive to the issue is a good starting point, followed by the development of some type of internal measuring device.

Understand that I am not suggesting that people blindly buy into a strategy without question. Good strategies can be modified and adjusted over time, based on feedback up and down the chain, as we discussed in Chapter 3. All I'm saying is that when your strategy calls for marching north and someone on your team insists on marching south, you've got a problem that has to be dealt with. On the other hand, if you're marching north and someone suggests you should be heading more to the northwest, it's probably worth stopping to analyze the situation.

In most organizations, there are a number of strong supporters of a strategy, a large number of fence sitters and a small number of detractors.

Fence sitters resemble supporters except they're never willing to jump off to one side or the other until they know which way the company is headed. Detractors are dangerous because they appeal more strongly to fence sitters than supporters do. That's why it's important to smoke out the detractors before launching the strategy.

Detractors don't necessarily have to be hunted down like terrorists and fired. What does have to happen, however, is some very frank discussion. Just as poor communication breeds dissent, good communication neutralizes it.

When meeting with a potential detractor, it's crucial to explain why their support is required and the consequences they face if they withhold it. Listening is also essential in these situations, and you should provide an opportunity for employees to express their specific concerns. If they aren't comfortable talking at that time, make it understood that you are open to discussing any of their thoughts or concerns at any time. And wind it up by telling them that while the choice is theirs, their support is a requirement of their continued employment.

These are four simple and fair conditions of employment. I've explained this to my management teams through the years and I use them as a coaching tool. How? Well, when a direct report brings me a problem he or she is having with one of their people, I frame the four conditions as questions. It usually allows us to isolate the root problem that needs to be resolved.

Make the four conditions your new "psychological contract" and you will find that you have fewer major personnel problems to deal with. And because the requirements of continued employment will be understood by all concerned, you also will minimize anxiety over job-security issues.

Chapter 9:
Time Is Money (Managing Your Time, The People You Manage And the People Who Manage You)

In This Chapter:
- Time Management
  - Managing Your Calendar
- Managing Paper and E-mail
- Managing Meetings
- Managing Subordinates
- Managing Your Boss
- Working with Your Peers

Why a chapter on organization and time management?

Isn't this mandatory learning for *junior* managers? By the time you became a full-fledged executive, didn't you have the whole organization and time management thing down?

But do you still have it down? The one mistake I have seen more senior managers make is allowing their time and organizational management skills to get rusty. Some assume these skills have become second nature. Others mistakenly believe they don't have the "luxury" of making time to manage their time the way they once did.

This would be akin to a seasoned pro football player rejecting the need to practice fundamental blocking and tackling skills once he got a huge contract.

The irony in all this is that senior managers have to be better at organization and time management then at any other point in their careers. Because success and failure are ultimately determined by *execution*, organization and time-management play a key role in managers' careers.

In this chapter we will discuss how to manage time, administer a staff, work with peers – and manage the boss.

Time Management

Stick to the basics when it comes to time management, beginning with a to-do list. I know many senior managers who don't use such a list, preferring instead to react to issues as they arise and select tasks to work on from memory. The upshot is they wind up juggling many tasks in their heads, act harried, and create emergencies when they fail to get out ahead of things.

I keep my to-do list on a PDA (personal digital assistant) but lower-tech products from outfits such as Day-Timers, Franklin/Covey Planner and Filofax accomplish the same thing. Lined paper with "To-Do" handwritten across the top can be just as effective – in fact, the act of copying unfinished tasks from one day's version of the list to the next makes them harder to forget.

Any to-do list should be based on what you need and want to get done, broken down to the task level. Make sure that you have a process in place for capturing tasks from mail, voice-mail and e-mail so they don't slip through the cracks.

The first day of each week, I pull out my to-do list and place a mark next to each item I want to accomplish that week. Then, each day, I select the tasks I want to finish that day – normally, between five and fifteen in number. Rather than tackling them in the same order I received them, I flag the tasks that must get done that day. If you find yourself with more than five must-do items for a given day, chances are they're not all must-do items.

As basic as this is, it's amazing how well it works. I look at my to-do list often and try to remain focused on it. By the end of the day, I usually have the must-do items accomplished.

The To-Do List as Stress Reliever: Anxiety-fed stress is the constant companion of the modern manager. Anxiety that commonly stems from a sense of being overwhelmed with things that have to be done can be substantially reduced simply by listing tasks and assigning completion dates to them. More often than not, the length of the true task list doesn't support that sense of being overwhelmed to begin with.

Managing Your Calendar

Whatever you do, never attempt to maintain more than one calendar. Keeping one calendar in your home, another on your desk, and a third in your briefcase only ensures that appointments will fall through the cracks when you forget to transfer everything from one calendar to another and another.

But you can fearlessly enjoy the benefits of multiple calendars by using a PDA and synchronizing it with your computer. By using e-mail software with a built-in calendar (Outlook and LotusNotes, to name two common ones), you can synchronize your PDA and allow others to schedule appointments for you without having to track you down to discuss them first (and the inevitable "phone tag" that entails).

My secretary accesses the same system to enter the details of my heavy travel schedule – hotels, flights, rental cars, confirmation numbers – the whole nine yards. This saves me from having to rummage through my briefcase in airports, taxis and hotel lobbies. It also enables me to beam my travel details into my wife's PDA, which is especially handy on those occasions when I head out on a two- or three-day trip without remembering to let her know how to reach me on the road. Fortunately for me, I have a very understanding wife with a Palm Pilot!

Managing Paper and E-mail

The goal when reviewing paper correspondence, e-mail and voicemail is to touch each one – whether constituted of wood fiber, electrons or pixels – no more than once. This means you never have to burn time finding items two or more times, or resorting the same list just to remind yourself what you have to do.

The way to do this is to execute one of the following five actions *the first time*:

1.   *Do It Now:* Applies to tasks that can be completed in two minutes or less. Examples include returning routine phone calls, writing three- or four-line e-mail replies or short notes that delegate the item to a subordinate. Do it now and get it off your desk.

2.   *Add It to Your To-Do List:* If it's written on a sheet of paper, file it in your To-Do folder. If it's part of a project, file it in an appropriately labeled project folder. If it's an e-mail, create a folder in your e-mail software called "To-Do" and move it there. If it's an e-mail that's part of a project, create an appropriately labeled folder in your e-mail system and put it there. (This also will keep your e-mail inbox from filling up.)

Regardless of where the item is stored, write the "To-Do" item on your To-Do list.

3. *Throw It Away:* Take no prisoners! If you don't need to act on it, or if you can count on someone else to save a copy, pitch it. Set your e-mail software to automatically delete messages after 90 days.

4. *Put It in Your File Pile:* My secretary does my filing using an elementary system utilizing A-Z hanging files. Each item to get filed goes into a separate manila folder, is labeled and filed. My secretary then enters the label name into an Excel file called "File Log," which serves as the index to my paper filing system. Before putting an item into my File Pile, I write the name of the folder I want it filed in on a sticky note as a guide for my secretary.

   I organize my computer a little differently. Rather than sorting items according to the software they are written on (Word, Excel or PowerPoint, for example) my files are saved in folders titled "Projects", "Personnel", "Reports" and "Miscellaneous." "Projects" is sorted into subfolders named for each project, "Personnel" into subfolders for each direct report, and so on.

5. *Send It to Someone Else To Do:* If the item requires follow up, suspense a note in your calendar to make sure it was done on the appointed day.

These are all simple activities that become second nature and can keep you from drowning in a sea of paper, pixels or electrons.

Managing Meetings

More than anything else, managers hate meetings. Why? Because even the rare necessary meeting is normally run poorly and lasts far too long. It's impossible to estimate how much time Corporate America wastes each year in unproductive meetings, but it must run into millions of hours. Imagine the productivity that could be released if even half of those sessions were eliminated.

When a meeting *is* necessary, it must be managed properly. The first step in managing a meeting is to identify the *type* of meeting it will be:

1. *Informational Meetings:* The purpose of an informational meeting is for you and your team to keep each other in the loop.

   I had a boss early in my career who called our Monday morning staff meetings "WGO (for What's Goin' On?) meetings." He would take no more than 10 minutes to bring us up to speed. Then each member of the staff had a maximum of five minutes to update the group on the things they needed to know. Smaller, follow-up action or project meetings would be scheduled for items that couldn't be covered in five minutes. Those meetings were capped at 45 minutes.

2. *Action Meetings:* Think of these as "who's going to do what" meetings. The outcome must be clearly defined tasks with clearly defined accountabilities, deliverables, deadlines and milestones. If an action meeting lasts longer than an hour, the participants weren't prepared going in.

3. *Project Meetings:* These are part informational and part action meetings, and are best for complex projects that require many participants. Project meetings should be divided into four segments: informational, task review and assignments, progress and objectives. They should be limited to an hour.

Pre-defining the length of a meeting keeps participants focused and ensures more effective use of time. An agenda that lists expectations for all attendees, accompanied by required reading materials always should be sent out in advance.

Managing Subordinates

The key to managing people is giving them clearly defined expectations and allowing them to participate in the definition of the specific accomplishments and goals their performance will be measured against in the coming 12 months. Subordinates should be allowed to develop their own action plans for achieving those goals according to mutually agreed upon deadlines.

Individual objectives should be reviewed together on a monthly basis to make sure they align with your larger objectives as well as their personal goals.

I'm often struck by a manager's inability to be open and straightforward in one-on-one communications. The tendency to avoid uncomfortable topics during interim reviews is unfair to employees and leaves them unprepared for bad news when their formal performance reviews roll around. It also leads to lawsuits after poor performers who weren't given regular, objective assessments of their performance are fired.

The one standard general managers should hold themselves to should be to ensure their direct reports are never surprised by what they hear at their performance reviews. General managers should also maintain an atmosphere in which 360° feedback is welcomed and confidentiality of professional or personal issues is guaranteed.

A Note on Secretaries: Your secretary is one of the most important members of your team. Because they routinely access other staffers' performance reviews and compensation information – not to mention legal documents, confidentiality agreements and more – you must be able to place complete trust in your secretary's integrity. When interviewing potential secretaries, be sure to explain how critical their ability to preserve confidential information will be, and that they will be evaluated on their performance in that respect.

Managing Your Boss

You read it right; it's essential to influence the individual who has the single greatest impact on the course of your career. Whatever else you do, make sure your boss is never surprised to hear information – good, bad or otherwise –you could have told her or him first but didn't. The same goes for information you should have known, but didn't. You should maintain this standard even with bosses that explode when they get bad news. Never allow their behavior to discourage you from doing what's best for the business. (In all likelihood, you'd only be postponing the explosion, anyway.)

By maintaining this standard, your boss will come to trust you for speaking the truth and keeping him or her in the loop – which enhances *their* standing in the company.

When discussing business tactics with your boss, feel free to disagree. Be sure, however, to remain within the scope of your professional expertise and never wander into personal issues. In those cases when the boss calls the shot his way, anyway, your job is to get behind the decision and work as hard as possible to implement it successfully. In this way, your boss will learn two valuable things: (1) you are not a "yes man" but rather a person of conviction, and (2) you're a team player who can be counted on to execute strategies when they are finalized.

What if you just can't stand your boss? As I see it, you have three options:

1. grin and bear it,

2. be alert for transfer opportunities within the company

3. fold your tent and move on to another company.

Take a hard look at the second and third options. It's a free country, so why let a bad boss derail your career and frustrate you? Make sure you don't get hung up thinking that options two and three aren't "fair," or that they amount to letting someone you don't respect run you out of town. For openers, who said life was fair? The important thing is to react strategically rather than impulsively, never burn your bridges, and leave the company with the impression of a mature general manager who doesn't let emotion interfere with sound judgment.

Working With Your Peers

Many managers forget the need to work strategically with people who manage other functions at the same level. If you want their support, especially in a company where infighting is condoned, the best way to ensure smooth working relationships is to develop solid interpersonal relationships with your peers.

Keeping them in the loop makes it much more likely that they will support your efforts and keep you advised of what they're doing in return. Communicate your business goals and objectives, and enlist their buy-in. Make sure you're not working at cross purposes. Seek out opportunities to help them, too!

Be straightforward in your dealings with difficult people. Don't pussyfoot around issues that involve yourself, your team members or your business objectives. Be direct but professional when asking them to express their concerns. You may be surprised at how disarming this can be, and how effectively it can de-escalate confrontational situations.

Some rules of thumb for peer relationships:

- Be open
- Don't fear or be distracted by office politics
- Share the credit for success
- Accept responsibility for failure
- Be the kind of peer you want your peers to be.

If you follow the advice offered in this chapter, your subordinates, boss and peers will see you as a WYSIWYG person – *what you see is what you get*. And you'll be amazed what it can do for your self-image and self-confidence.

Life Skills

The Lost Art of General Management

Chapter 10:
Advancing Your Career

In This Chapter:

- Developing Your Skills
- Networking
  - Internal Networking
  - External Networking
  - Networking Tips
- Actively Seeking New Employment
  - Something Else to Avoid: Job Brokers
  - The Four Methods of Conducting a Job Search

I assume that one of the main reasons you're reading this book is to find useful ideas and tools that will make you more effective in your job and advance your career. It's only human nature to have ambition.

Healthy ambition can lead you to success in life. On the other hand, "unhealthy" ambition – the kind that leads to putting yourself ahead of the team or putting your success ahead of the company – could derail your career. The four conditions of employment I discussed in an earlier chapter provide a good tool to ensure that your ambition is a catalyst for advancement, not a deterrent to it.

Healthy ambition means maximizing opportunities when they arise and managing your career proactively. "I'd rather be lucky than good" may be a clever saying but it has no place in the context of a career. Any successful person will tell you they got where they are by creating their own luck – which means recognizing opportunities and acting upon them.

There are three ways to advance your career:

1. Develop your skills
2. Network
3. Seek new employment

Developing Your Skills

One of the best ways to grow your skills is to choose a non-traditional career path. This can be particularly effective if you work for a large publicly traded company where non-traditional positions are more apt to be noticed by senior managers and your work will be more visible. Also, non-traditional jobs tend to be assigned broader responsibilities sooner, which will give you experience that will put you ahead of your peers.

Real World Story No. 21

I was hired off the college campus by Armstrong World Industries in 1984 and went into their sales training program. During this training we were taught the traditional career path in sales, which features sequential promotions to assistant regional sales manager, regional sales manager, national sales (or marketing) manager and then, for the very best, divisional vice president. It was a competitive environment, and all the hotshots who came in from the college training program were vying for their first promotion.

While I held three different outside sales assignments, some of my peers were already being promoted to assistant regional sales managers. I wondered how you got on the "list" and how to keep your career moving. I feared that if I didn't get to that next rung of the ladder soon, my career at Armstrong would be limited. Well, at about that time, Armstrong purchased a small subsidiary company that specialized in high-end architectural products. The subsidiary only sold through fully commissioned independent sales agents, but the division vice president wondered if a salaried Armstrong sales person also could succeed in that type of environment. A positive outcome could change the way Armstrong organized its sales force. When I learned of this, I jumped at the chance and became the subsidiary's first "in-house" sales person.

My peers thought it was insane to remain in sales at a small subsidiary rather than moving into management. But I rolled the dice and a year later I was promoted to product manager of this subsidiary – reporting directly to its president. Two years later, I was offered the position of marketing manager for Armstrong's Canadian company because I was literally the only person with the necessary product-marketing background.

Again, my peers thought I was nuts. Wasn't Canada out of the parent company's mainstream? Maybe so, but I learned a lot about international business and how to deal in different cultural environments. This experience in turn led to a promotion as the head of their Latin American business.

By this time I was used to having my career judgment questioned. But I had also seen the value of selecting the road less taken – a trait that has rewarded my career several more times, leading to my present position as a vice president at Worthington Industries. Had I not experienced the benefits of non-traditional assignments early in my career, it's doubtful I would have accumulated the experience and confidence that have enabled me to be where I am today – and will be in the future.

Don't settle for the traditional career path at your company when the non-traditional offers experience that others in your company don't have. If that isn't an option, volunteering for special projects is another good way to diversify your career development.

Another is through executive education. My employers have given me the opportunity to attend a number of exec ed programs at prominent schools such as Stanford, Penn State and Harvard, and I have paid for other programs out of my own pocket. If your company doesn't pay for exec ed, you should budget it for yourself once a year or once every other year.

Seminars offer another path to education. Many seminars don't cost much and can be found on consultants' websites. Many consultants offer free seminars as a way of showing off their wares. As a matter of fact, that's how I met the Strategic Pricing Group I referred to in Chapter 8. Not only did I learn something valuable at their seminar, I hired them to put on a private seminar for all of our sales managers and marketing managers, which was a cost- effective way of educating my people.

Finally, don't overlook books. If you find this book helpful, go to www.robwaite.com for a recommended reading list and other resources.

Networking

Another way to advance your career is through networking – *real* networking, as contrasted with shameless self-promotion and brownnosing! Real networks are earned through relationships established using the norm of reciprocity.

The norm of reciprocity is an interesting little study in psychology. It refers to the strong need many people feel to return a favor in order to discharge a debt. A person who is networking in the truest sense, then, is always on the lookout for opportunities to do favors for others that count as credits they feel obliged to pay back as part of the networking process. In this sense, Don Vito Corleone was the ultimate networker.

Brian Tracy, the noted motivational speaker and author, has a more honorable view than Don Corleone: "Successful people are always looking for opportunities to help others," he said. "Unsuccessful people are always asking, 'What's in it for me?'"

Internal Networking

Internal networking must be done sensitively to avoid the impression of self promotion or brownnosing. The important thing is remember the golden rule of networking – doing what you can for the other guy.

Real World Story No. 22

Earlier in this chapter I referred to the risk I took of finding myself out of the mainstream by accepting a position in Canada. Because I was concerned about this, I took advantage of quarterly visits to our Pennsylvania headquarters for regularly scheduled meetings to briefly stop and meet with no fewer than 15 people who impacted my ability to conduct business in Canada and, therefore, impacted my career.

What could I do for these people? Keep them up to date about what was going on in Canada, for the most part. Realizing that most people don't get updated by reading formal reports, I would swing in and spend 10 or 15 minutes bringing them up to speed. In this way, I made it possible for them to have the information they needed to satisfy any potential inquiry from the divisional vice president about the Canadian business.

After a few of these visits, I had no problem picking up the phone and getting immediate help when I needed it. Also, people at the head office probably got to know me better than if I had spent the same amount of time in the U.S. as a sales manager.

External Networking

The key to external networking is to avoid becoming trapped inside a closed loop. I'm referring here to the importance of branching out to people beyond your industry or function. Unless you do, you'll have only a narrow circle to call upon when needed. By branching out and developing a broader network, you'll have access not only to the contacts you made directly, but also to *their* contacts.

Your external network can be derived from friends, social contacts, people you've met on the golf course, whatever. Everyone you meet is a potential network contact – as long as you remember the importance of looking out to find ways to help them.

Real World Story No. 23

I discovered my current position – vice president-commercial of Worthington Industries' Dietrich Industries Division – through networking. This opportunity would never have been on my radar screen otherwise, and I would never have been on Worthington's.

I had spoken confidentially with a well-placed individual in the building materials industry – a person I had been networking with for about three years – to let him know that I was beginning to seek a new opportunity. He asked me what I was thinking about and I described the kind of job I was hoping to land.

Just a week or two later, the president of Dietrich Industries, who had recently been promoted out of the position I have now, happened to mention his need to fill that job to the person in my network. He got us together, and the rest, as they say, is history. Some might call that "luck," but if it was, it was luck that I made for myself.

A Caution About "Networking Events"

Beware of contrived events where the unemployed "network" among themselves. The theory behind them is that individuals can exchange information about jobs they have left or heard about while conducting their own job searches. The truth is that no one is looking out for the other guy at these events, but rather looking desperately for someone who can help *them*. This isn't networking so much as it is a support group.

Networking Tips

Demonstrating sincere interest in individuals is a good way to begin cultivating networking contacts. Ask them what they do, who they work for and where they're from. Get a sense of their personality type. Note the sports teams they follow and where their kids go to school. Once you do, track the information in your PDA or your e-mail contact manager so you don't have to rely on your memory.

Later, when you receive information you feel would be useful to that person, contact them and pass it along.

Real World Story No. 24

A good friend and neighbor of mine decided to leave his job with a large publicly traded company rather than accept a move to another location. After several moves, and with a kid halfway through high school, he thought it best for his family to negotiate a package and leave his company. As he was telling me about this, I thought of at least three people who might know of potential opportunities for him.

Two of them happened to live in our neighborhood also, and although my friend knew them from the bimonthly dinner parties we hold in the community, he had no idea they could help him find a job. I guess it was understandable – he had been with the same company for more than 20 years and hadn't developed his networking skills. Today, he's an expert at it.

I also have found my attorney, accountant and doctors through a form of networking that amounts to asking people I trust for their recommendations.

Once again, networking is a tool that used in the proper spirit – which is to say, the spirit of finding ways to help others – will not only help you locate a promising job, it also can make you a better friend and neighbor.

Actively Seeking New Employment

Sometimes, the best way or the only way to advance your career is to look for new opportunities elsewhere. Be careful, however! Just because the going may be tough in your current role or you may be upset about one thing or another, make sure you weigh the good against the bad before leaving.

I have hired many executives and helped an even greater number of friends and network contacts search for new jobs. I'm always surprised at how little most of them know about the job-search process itself. Compounding their lack of knowledge is usually a lack of preparation.

The job market for executives is difficult today and will likely remain difficult for years to come. Therefore, the executive seeking a new opportunity has to be more knowledgeable and better prepared than at any time in the past.

Having moved into senior positions at three large companies before age forty gained me a bit of notoriety among my friends and network contacts – particularly because I wasn't recruited for any of them. Instead, I located these positions through an methodical job search that combined all four of the search techniques I'll list in this section.

The first thing you need to ensure when embarking on an executive job search is that you accept the personal responsibility for the entire process. A job search is one of the most important activities you will undertake, so the burden for success or failure must rest squarely on your shoulders. The reason I am so emphatic about this is that far too many people accept one or both of the following misconceptions:

The first misconception is that the outplacement consultant is responsible for getting you a job. The second misconception is that the resume writer and distribution service you hired will find you a job. These things *could* happen, but *don't count on it!* It is much more likely that you will have wasted time and money by not taking full responsibility for your search.

If your company provided an outplacement service for you, push them hard because they're getting paid whether you find a job or not. Even better, try negotiating an arrangement with your former employer in which they will give you an amount in cash equal to what they would pay the outplacement service. You are much more likely to focus the money in ways that address your needs.

As you have gathered, I am not a big fan of outplacement services. I compare executives going through outplacement to the walking dead. Outplacement is reminiscent of poorly conceived government entitlement programs that drain any motivation from people who are forced to rely on them.

This isn't surprising, given that most of the executives who mix in outplacement have been pushed out of their jobs. They tend to be bitter, and feel they are owed a new job by the outplacement firm. The smartest thing you can do is to get over it as quickly as you can. Instead of becoming bitter, look forward and focus on what is important to you and your family. Bad things happen to good people and good companies, but you can control your reaction to the situation. Being a savvy and knowledgeable job seeker can help you preserve your health while opening up better opportunities for you.

Something Else to Avoid: Job Brokers

Happiness isn't the only thing that money can't buy; it can't buy you a job, either. I recommend avoiding resume-distribution firms with wild claims of success and people who purport to broker jobs in exchange for a fee. You can learn to do the same things yourself with a little time and effort, while saving yourself a great deal of money.

The reality is that any job search starts and ends with you. You need to do the work, anyway. The resume writer needs you to provide a lot of information about yourself. The distribution firm will require you to select the companies they send your resume to. And the brokers I mentioned are essentially nothing more than high-priced coaches.

It's important to realize that an executive job search is a numbers game. Because you're approaching the narrowest point of the pyramid, where demand for executive positions far outstrips the supply, your resume has to arrive at the moment a company or recruiter is looking for your particular skill and experience. Because statistics say you'll get very few hits, you must get up to bat as often as possible.

Too many executives delude themselves into believing the process is easier than it really is. They think that once they get their name out there and their resume reaches 30 companies or so, the world will beat a path to their door. But the process is much tougher than that.

Also, as you progress up the career ladder, less emphasis is placed on your functional skills in the hiring process. For instance, the first thing the hiring executive will want to assess is whether you are the kind of person they want to work with. If he or she doesn't have a good feel for you personally, it will be difficult for you to win them over. This may seem unfair, but it's only human nature.

Next in importance are your functional skills, and you'll be asked to list specific successes and experience that demonstrate your ability to perform the position.

Following that is your compatibility with the company's culture and environment. Learn as much as you can about the company's culture. If you're a numbers-driven, task-oriented manager, a nurturing consensus-driven culture wouldn't be a good fit. And it makes no sense to try to work where you don't fit in.

Another thing the hiring executive will be evaluating is whether or not you will be a risky hire. A bad hiring decision costs significant time and money for the company. If the job represents a big step from your previous one, or if you're moving to a new industry, the element of risk increases.

Once you know what's likely to go through the mind of the hiring executive, you can better prepare yourself to deal with both spoken and unspoken objections. But the bottom line issue is always the same: will you bring value to the company that far exceeds the compensation they will pay you? You must focus the whole job-search process on isolating opportunities that enable you to maximize the value you can deliver.

Many executives have contacted me seeking employment and have started by telling me what they thought they deserved and were worth. You know what? I couldn't care less. If they're not interested in selling me on the value they can deliver *first*, why should I be interested in what they want?

If the hiring executive is convinced of the value that you can deliver, you will likely get an offer that is actually *higher* than you felt you "deserved." Once the company decides it wants you, it is not going to let an additional $10,000, $20,000 or even $50,000 in compensation stand in the way of hiring you. But you have to unequivocally demonstrate tangible value that you can for sure deliver.

I've often been asked how long a search should be expected to take. While there's no reliable answer to that question, most people at the six-figure level begin to land positions between the sixth and twelfth months. It could take much less time for you, but again, don't count on it. Rather, plan on a solid year of work conducting your job search and you may be pleasantly surprised rather than discouraged if nothing happens in the first month or two. In other words, plan for the worst and hope for the best.

If you are currently employed, you will have to have the discipline required to devote evening, weekend and vacation time to your search. But I would stop short of leaving your current job to look full time for your new opportunity because having a job when interviewing increases your perceived value.

If you are currently unemployed don't waste any time. Get started right away. Don't let anyone convince you to take a month off to clear your head or anything like that. Get the forward momentum going!

Also, be open to relocation. The wider the geography you're willing to move within, the better your odds in the numbers game. Besides, relocation can be a growing experience for both you and your family. It's not easy, but it is rewarding. I've lived and worked on three continents and in several cities in the U.S. and Canada. I know I've benefited from the experience – as have my wife and kids.

It's critically important to stay motivated throughout the process. Getting turned down 99 percent of the time (literally) can get you down, so remember that it only takes one "you're hired" to make it all worthwhile. Don't take rejection personally because 95 percent of the turndowns you receive are due to the absence of an open executive position suited to you at the time, rather than your qualities. And remember that while searching for a job is a highly personal and emotional experience for you, it's just part of the job for the hiring executive or recruiter.

The Four Methods of Conducting a Job Search

There are four main methods of searching for your six-figure position:

1. Direct mail to executive recruiters
2. Direct mail to employers, including venture-capital firms that may be looking to change the management of any of their portfolio companies
3. Networking – which will involve people you know both directly and indirectly
4. Internet job banks.

You will need to use a combination of all four methodologies to ensure success. As a matter of fact, during my last job search, I ended up with job offers through all of them.

Throughout this book I recommend books and resources offered by other people to help you develop your skills in a particular area of management. In this case, I will recommend my own product, the CD-based seminar "The Six Figure Job Search." The program is geared to managers who are at or approaching six-figure base pay. The seminar takes you through the entire job search process from planning your campaign to negotiating the offer. For more information, go to www.sixfigurejobsearch.com.

Chapter 11:
Work-Life Balance

In This Chapter:

- Tools for Maintaining Balance
- Finding Time
- Expanding Your Horizons
- The Value of Lifelong Interests and Purposefulness
- Don't Forget the Kids!
- Gut-Check Your Way Into Balance

Do we work to live or do we live to work?

I'm sure you've heard people ask this question from time to time. The answer is "both." We need to work in order to provide for ourselves and our families. We also work for personal fulfillment. All humans need the sense of accomplishment that comes from a job well done.

Things go awry when our personal and working lives go out of balance. Not that it's possible to maintain a state of equilibrium at all times; sometimes it's necessary to spend a period of time highly immersed in one area of your life or the other. The operative phrase is *a period of time*.

Let's face it; the working world is much more demanding than it ever has been. In the white-collar world, hours worked per week have been creeping up and days of vacation taken have been shrinking.

So what's a person to do?

Tools for Maintaining Balance

To maintain balance, I recommend that you develop specific goals and priorities set around areas of your life that are important to you. Don't just say, "I want to spend more time with my kids." You have to be much more specific if you are going to succeed. And you already have the tools for doing it; the same ones we discussed in the earlier chapter on managing time.

What are your personal objectives or goals for the day, week, month or year? Are you scheduling time for your family, friends, hobbies, or health (exercise and doctor visits, for example)?

Finding Time

By applying the same principles, you will be able to wring out more time for your personal life and actually accomplish those person plans rather than just talking about them.

Real World Story No. 25

I am the father of three daughters, a husband, a gainfully employed executive of a large company, an author and a public speaker. Time is a precious commodity to me – one that I take care to manage precisely.

My wife and I actually sit down to do weekly planning together. After all, she depends on me to free up time for her as much as I depend on her to help me – though I have to admit that she does most of the heavy lifting for the family.

We plan two family vacations a year and get them on the calendar in January, if we can. I make sure that my staff and my boss also have those dates on their calendars so that last-minute priorities don't suddenly get in the way. I've had to shave a day or two here and there from time to time due to a sudden business situation such as an acquisition opportunity. But had I not scheduled the vacation time early and communicated it, odds are the whole vacation would have gone down the drain.

Since I travel so much, when I am in town I make sure I'm home by six or six thirty to have dinner with the family. A lot is discussed at the dinner table in our house, so I'm always happy to be there.

It's always a struggle to find time for exercise. Because the only reliable time I have for exercise is early in the morning, I get up at 5:30 am. My exercise companion is Benny, our Vizsla. Benny and I walk one of three different routes that range from 30 minutes to one and a half hours. The route we select depends on when I have to get to the office and the weather. If I could teach Benny how to lift weights, I probably would do that more often, too.

These walks are also productive for me. I first start by thinking about the top five things I need to get done at work that day. Also, this book was conceived, outlined and half written (in my head) during my morning constitutionals. Had I been able to teach Benny to take dictation, this book would have been done much sooner!

The point is, you can find time to get things done by using a little imagination. If you travel a lot, the airport can become your office away from the office with the correct planning. Buying a membership to a major airline's club is money (or inflight mileage credits) very well spent for this purpose. The clubs have everything you need to plug in and comfortably get connected with the business world. You'll be thankful for the investment with the first major flight delay you experience after joining.

Expanding Your Horizons

Feeding your mind also is important. While most executives will spend most of their learning time reading business books and periodicals and learning about their company and their products, it is also wise to broaden your horizons for the pure joy of learning.

I'm a history nut. I particularly enjoy studying the Revolutionary War Era and the Space Race. I know other executives who are into music or the theater. All of this helps round out your perspective and builds your mind.

My historical studies have also helped me greatly in business. Both the American Revolution and the competition for supremacy in space required overcoming strong odds. The leaders in each of these eras had to think and act like general managers. Much that we learn from the study of history can be applied to our daily lives. And the opposite is true, per the George Santayana quote I cited earlier: "Those who ignore history are doomed to repeat it."

Real World Story No. 26

"Houston, we have a problem!" Remember that line from the movie *Apollo 13*? Or if you are old enough, you may remember that line from the NASA rebroadcast of transmissions from Apollo 13 on April 13, 1970.

About four years ago, the company I worked for was going through a particularly tough time. Nothing that couldn't be overcome, but the troops were becoming a little disheartened and I could tell that a few were considering choosing failure as an option.

Because I was old enough to remember 1970 (I was 8 years old) and having studied three different books and the movie based on the Apollo 13 saga, I thought my team could benefit from hearing from someone who did not choose failure as an option. I was able to get Fred Haise, the Lunar Module Pilot on Apollo 13, to speak to our group.

Fred talked about how the three-man crew needed to react to the situation quickly without panicking, how they had to trust others at NASA to do their part and how they needed to stay focused on working the problem and not get overwhelmed by its severity. He was soft spoken and mild in manner... and highly pragmatic. Fred's talk was a true inspiration to everyone and he tipped the momentum in the organization back to an orientation towards success.

The Value of Life-long Interests and Purposefulness

Hobbies and interests outside of work are particularly important. Because they offer escape that helps refresh and revitalize you both physically and mentally, they also enable you to get more out of the time you do spend at work.

Golfing on the weekend with your boss or clients is *not* going to accomplish this. When you do this, you are still on duty and you won't get the full benefit of the time spent away from the office. On the other hand, an enjoyable round of golf with friends who will laugh with you when you shank your ball into the lake provides an opportunity to refresh and revitalize.

Having outside interests is critical to you later in life as well. There is nothing sadder than a person who has had no life outside work who finds little enjoyment in retirement. "Get a life" is good advice for people in this category.

My father is probably the best example of how to do it right. He put himself in the position of being able to retire from fulltime work in his mid-fifties. He had always invested time in exercise, fishing, boating, golfing and investments. The investments were more of a hobby than a job, but they helped make it possible for him to retire young.

He is now in his mid-seventies and has never once wished he was back at work. He spends his summers fishing at the New Jersey shore and his winters playing golf in Florida.

On Sundays when we talk, after we discuss the kids and Philadelphia's sports teams, we talk about the stock market and the right places to invest. Having this type of purposeful life has kept him significantly younger than most men his age.

Don't Forget the Kids!

Just about every business person I know who is also a parent talks about the need to spend more time with their kids. For me, the most important thing is that my teenage daughters still open up and talk with my wife and me. This is the key performance indicator by which we evaluate our parenting.

When my daughters stop talking about boyfriends, school or what's on their minds, its time to dig in and find out what's going on. To get my kids to talk, I have to choose the timing properly. Typically in the car, over dinner or just while doing chores together, I can get them to open up. I also call home every night when I'm on the road. It's no secret and hardly sexist to suggest that girls like to talk on the phone. Sometimes I get more information about what's going on in their lives over the phone when I'm away than face-to-face at home, especially since formal sit-downs tend to get their defenses up (or anyone's, for that matter).

Gut-Check Your Way Into Balance

Quite often, your gut instinct can be a more reliable measure of work-life balance than your reasoning mind. Most of us tend to rationalize an imbalance when we look at things from a "logical" perspective. Why? Because we either don't want to have to face issues in certain areas of our lives or because we're doing what we think we should be doing according to some unrealistic standard.

It pays to take a few minutes every week to clear your head, review your business and personal lives – and listen to what your gut has to say.

Chapter 12:
Managing Stress

In This Chapter:
- What's Wellness?
- You Are What You Eat
  - Avoiding the D-Word (Dieting)
  - Eating Healthy in a Fast-Paced World
- Techniques for Managing Stress
  - Exercise
  - Nutrition
  - Meditation
  - Visualization
  - Deep Breathing
  - Alcohol as Stress Reliever
- Resilience
- Effective Exercise
  - The Benefits of Exercising Regularly
  - Exercising When There's No Time to Exercise
  - Practical Exercise Tips

Stress is the constant companion of the modern manager. While stress has gotten a bad rap, it is not an inherently injurious thing. Dr. Hans Selye, the Hungarian endocrinologist who introduced the concept of stress in the 1930s, identified both beneficial ("eustress") and harmful ("distress") varieties of stress.

To cut short a potential sidetrack in the making here, the only important thing to remember is that stress was an upshot of Dr. Selye's "General Adaptation Syndrome," which accounted for the fact that the same events generate different physiological changes in people depending on their adaptability at the time.

The implications for managers are immense. The ability to effectively manage the inevitable stresses of one's job not only is critical to short-term performance, it also has a significant effect on an individual's career and life in general over the long haul. Managers who can deal with stressful situations capably are much more likely to move up the ladder than those who are dominated by it. These are people who are easy to spot because they tend to look fit, react alertly, have a more positive outlook and seem comfortable in their surroundings. That's because the ability to deal with stress is strongly linked to the physical and mental health of any individual. In this context, "health" is actually a state of wellness – a condition that is determined by long-range lifestyle choices involving diet, exercise and more. We're not talking about pumping iron here or drinking carrot juice from a blender. We're talking about a pattern of sensible decisions that keeps the mind and body strong and adaptable to stress.

In a sense, this chapter could as easily have been placed first, rather than last in my book. Because if you're perceived as someone who wilts or bounces off the walls when the going gets rough, you ain't gonna make it on the job regardless of how much you know.

What's Wellness?

Since this chapter of the book was beyond my direct area of expertise, I turned to a bona fide expert resource in the field, Pittsburgh-based Highmark, Inc. Primarily a health insurer, Highmark has been out in front of the wellness concept for decades and has dedicated itself to understanding and promoting wellness for the benefit of its customers and the general public. Tina Palaggo-Toy, who heads up the company's health-promotion efforts, explained what wellness is – and isn't.

"We tend to think of health only in the physical realm, so we tend to define health as the absence of disease," she explains. But wellness is much more than that; it's a continuum that takes health to the next level because it enables people to feel good, have more joy in their lives, move their bodies comfortably and with strength – and enjoy an excellent quality of life."

Wellness recognizes that humans are holistic beings, and as such need to make good choices on many things that affect their health. For example, the things we put into our bodies affect us emotionally as well as physically. They also largely determine our body weight, which in turn has significant implications for development of chronic diseases such as diabetes and heart disease – and on the strength of the immune system.

You Are What You Eat

But diet also has a significant impact on shorter-term adaptability – as manifested in constantly changing energy levels. Some foods are energy-producing foods whereas others are energy-draining. Some enhance mental acuity while others can make a person fuzzy. Some lift us up naturally and others only make us sluggish.

Palaggo-Toy invokes the relatively new concept of "presenteeism" to explain the ramifications for businesses and businesspeople. "Diet alone won't determine whether or not a person goes to work on any given day, but it will affect job performance. Just because a person is at work, it doesn't mean they're productive."

Asked for a rule of thumb that differentiates energy-producing from energy-draining foods, Palaggo-Toy recommends "foods from the earth," such as fruits, beans and other vegetables, which contain complex carbohydrates and promote the production of seratonin in the body. At the opposite pole are candy bars – simple carbohydrates that temporarily increase energy levels but rapidly lead to sluggishness and even depression as blood-sugar levels drop dramatically.

Foods that are high in Omega-3 fatty acids, such as fish and nuts, actually reduce depression and improve mental acuity. Other beneficial foods include those made from whole grains rather than refined grains; multi-grain breads, as opposed to white bread, for example. Multi-grain pastas also are easy to find these days, as is brown rice. Beans, nuts and legumes also are multi-grain foods. Olive oil is a good choice, as are lean sources of protein such as fish and soy-based foods.

Avoiding the D-Word (Dieting)

With the exception of persons having overarching medical conditions, Palaggo-Toy recommends against the adoption of highly restrictive diets – such as the low-carbohyrdrate "Atkins Diet" that seems to reappear on the horizon like Halley's Comet from time to time. "You should never adopt a program that prevents you from eating certain food groups," she cautions. "How can you not eat fruits?" It is characteristic of these diets, she explains, that their benefits end after a year, often as the result of health problems associated with one form of nutrition deprivation or another.

The inherent shortcomings of dieting only emphasize the advantages of adopting healthy long-range lifestyle modifications. The very fact that diets are not sustainable – in fact, people only follow diets for 42 days on average – is all one really needs to know. But it's worse than that, because diet-induced weight loss inevitably results from loss of needed muscle tissue rather than fat.

Palaggo-Toy says *sustainability* is the key to a healthy eating plan. "I tell people to follow the '80/20 Rule.' If you eat sensibly 80 percent of the time and make good choices, you will feel better, be lighter, remember things better and have more energy." She goes on to say that succumbing to the lure of the occasional cheeseburger and fries doesn't mean a person has "failed" under the 80/20 principle.

Eating Healthy In a Fast-Paced World

It takes a little planning, but it's not difficult to maintain a sensible eating program regardless of the hours you work or the other demands on your time. The idea is to think ahead and be mindful of the question, "what do I want to put in my body?" Not only will this result in more fruitful (pun entirely intended) supermarket sorties where meals are concerned, it also will ensure that apples or celery and carrots are available as alternatives to chips and cheese doodles when the munchies strike.

One practical solution to the problem of cooking healthy meals quickly is preparing meals in advance on weekends and freezing one- or two-person portions to be warmed up in the microwave during the week.

Here are few others:

- Although frozen vegetables aren't as good for you as fresh ones, they're still better than canned and they cook faster

- Keep the pantry stocked with relatively healthy foods that have a long shelf life, such as soups and tuna fish

- Investigate new types of snack foods that actually taste good as well as having nutritive value, like string cheese and whole-grain crackers
- Don't go food shopping when you're hungry

Techniques for Managing Stress

As is the case with several other health conditions, the first step in coping with stress is recognizing that you're afflicted by it. Here are some of the classic tell-tale signs:

- poor concentration or a lack of focus
- irritability (unstressed people don't flip the bird at every other stoplight)
- restlessness
- appetite changes (in either direction)
- muscle pain, especially between the shoulder blades and forehead
- self-medicating (alcohol, drugs, cigarettes) for a quick fix
- cynicism, low morale and declining job satisfaction

Fortunately, there are a number of effective ways for reducing or eliminating stress – some of which can be done in the work setting. Tina Palaggo-Toy advises that there's no one "best" way for coping with stress, but rather the method that works best for any given person.

Exercise

Exercise physiologists and wellness experts always differentiate between "exercise" on the one hand and "activity" on the other. Just being actively engaged in a physical activity (bowling comes to mind) may burn calories, but it won't necessarily bring out the physiological changes that will better enable the body to cope with stress. For that, a person must engage in exercise that uses the large-muscle groups and improves cardiovascular capacity. Examples are running (or walking) and swimming. Also, after about 35 minutes of cardiovascular exercise, endorphins are released into the bloodstream, which are sort of like nature's Prozac.

Nutrition

Again, the goal is to prevent blood-sugar levels from dropping too low to help the body deal effectively with stress. Never go three hours or longer without eating – even if it's just a snack.

Meditation

The benefits of meditation have gained wide popular acceptance in the past decade. The perception of meditation as the exclusive practice of Tibetan monks and mystic, Rasputin-like characters has been replaced with the increasingly familiar site of executives taking 20 minutes in their offices to focus on their breathing and recite a mantra with the lights dimmed.

Entering "how to meditate" into an Internet search engine turns up a variety of options. My advice is to give it a try, even if the idea of meditating seems a little too New Age to you. Believe me, "real" business people *do* practice meditation!

Visualization

Not to be confused with "daydreaming," visualization provides a deliberate means of removing oneself from a stressful situation through conjuring up images of tranquil, pleasurable experiences. Looking at snapshots taken on vacations is a good way for abstract-challenged people to get the process going.

Deep Breathing

Rapid, shallow breathing is one of the classic physiological manifestations of stress – an upshot of the "fight or flight" reaction identified by Dr. Selye in the thirties. By shutting one's eyes and breathing in a slow, deliberate manner from the stomach up through the chest, the body relaxes and stress is reduced.

Other tips for managing stress include:

- eating breakfast;
- lifestyle-management activities such as listening to music or calling a friend;
- walking away from stressful situations;

- negotiating deadlines that recognize what you can and can't do
- invoking humor to turn the tables on stress.

Palaggo-Toy also recommends the programs of the Institute of HeartMath, a California-based nonprofit group that has developed techniques for dealing with stress and negative emotions. The group's interactive software-based "Freeze-Framer" program encourages people to deliberately shift to positive emotions such as caring or compassion when stressed because doing so stimulates changes in the body that lower blood pressure, increase calmness and control, and release anti-aging hormones. More information is available at http://heartmath.org/education/freeze-framer/freeze-framer-adult.html.

Alcohol As Stress Reliever

Almost everyone drinks and there's nothing wrong with drinking *per se*. Some recent studies have even suggested that drinking in moderation may have some healthful effects. But by the same token, we've come a long way from the day when "being able to hold your liquor" was actually considered a business skill and deals were sealed over three martinis.

I've known a few really talented and hard-working people whose promising careers unfortunately were derailed by intemperate alcohol use. In today's environment, employees who have earned the reputation of a "drinker" are viewed as potential liabilities for a wide variety of reasons ranging from rising health insurance premiums, liability claims and integrity problems to simply being potential sources of embarrassment. In my case, while I enjoy going out with friends and colleagues "for drinks," it's the camaraderie and fun, rather than the alcohol, that ultimately serve to relieve my stress. If you find it to be the other way around, your drinking is actually counterproductive.

Resilience

Perhaps the most intriguing concept Tina Palaggo-Toy shared with me that suits the needs of general managers is *resilience*. She defines it as the ability to persevere and adapt to situations – a critical ability for anyone who works for someone else and is therefore unable to control the forces that determine success or failure.

Resilience in this context is a quality that is made up of 10 separate and distinct traits that can be viewed as skills or talents in the context of rediscovering the art of general management. Examine these as you did the basic skill set I outlined back in the first chapter, and determine the ones that you need to improve on before you can achieve a state of resilience.

- *The ability to be decisive:* do you act in a way that's consistent with the influence associated with your position – or do you betray a sense of helplessness?

- *A sense of purpose:* do your actions support the performance indicators established for your position and your department, or do you do things for the sake of looking busy?

- *Adherence to values:* are you able to list the values you bring to your work – and are you consistently faithful to them?

- *Creativity:* when traditional methods for accomplishing your assigned tasks prove ineffective, are you able to "call an audible" and come up with a new approach that works?

- *Self-care:* do you keep yourself in shape mentally and physically to overcome the stresses that you must deal with?

- *Humor:* do you have the ability to laugh at ridiculous odds and put things into perspective, or would people say of you "he takes himself way too seriously?"

- *Acting responsibly:* are you the kind of manager who shoulders the blame when things go awry – or is the phrase "I screwed up" totally beyond your vocabulary?

- *Seeking support:* are you comfortable asking others for help, advice and mentoring – or do you consider that a sign of weakness?

- *Optimism:* Do you focus on achieving the things that you can do – or is it just as acceptable to consider yourself the victim of forces beyond your control?

Exercise

Tina Palaggo-Toy is probably understating the truth when she says that exercise has "hundreds of thousands" of benefits. In addition to the advantages that follow, I'll add this: To advance your career and increase your value to your family as well as yourself, you must have both energy and self-esteem. Exercise will help you gain both.

The Benefits of Following a Regular Exercise Program:

- reduces the risk of chronic health conditions such as coronary artery disease and diabetes;
- is the key to effective weight management when it combines strength training and calorie-burning activities
- strengthens emotional as well as physical health, and benefits the mind through the release of Beta-endorphins
- increases the amount of oxygen that goes to every cell of the body, generating additional energy, endurance and productivity
- reduces low-back pain through the strengthening of abdominal and lower back muscles
- reduces tension through the stretching of hamstring muscles, which also improves focus and productivity

Exercising When There's No Time to Exercise

The image of the executive coming to work with a squash racquet under his or her arm in anticipation of the daily match at the club has gone the way of the three-martini lunch. Who the hell has time for that? As I mentioned in the chapter on work/life balance, my daily exercise often is limited to my morning walks with the family dog, Benny. While I would prefer to visit the gym two or three times a week, it's ridiculous to imagine how I could carve the time out to do that. That's why I was somewhat relieved to hear Palaggo-Toy's advice on exercising when it's impossible to maintain the "ideal" schedule.

She explains that research has shown the benefits of exercise are essentially cumulative – in other words, a little here and a little there adds up at the end of the day. That being the case, the trick is to evaluate the routine activities you perform with an eye to deriving the maximum exercise benefit from them. An obvious example is taking the stairs instead of an elevator as often as possible. Going for a walk at lunchtime is another.

I especially like the suggestion of parking at the far end of the parking lot from the mall entrance so you wind up walking as far as possible.

Palaggo-Toy suggests acquiring a pedometer – a device that counts the number of steps you take over a given period of time – and setting the goal of reaching 10,000 steps per day. Here's where knowing that the benefits of exercise are cumulative is important: 10,000 steps is the equivalent of between four and five miles. Most people who don't have time to dedicate to a five-mile walk every day almost surely could derive the same benefit by reengineering their daily foot-traffic patterns.

Practical Exercise Tips

Here are a few other recommendations related to exercise:

Set SMART goals (Specific, Measurable, Adaptable, Realistic and Timely) as opposed to goals that sound like "I want to lose some weight."

Use the "talk but not sing" rule to regulate the intensity of your workouts.

Try to exercise at least 20 minutes a day – regardless of the form the exercise takes. The American Academy of Sports Medicine recommends between 20 and 60 minutes, according to Palaggo-Toy.

Shoot for between two and three sessions of strength training during the week, always allowing a day between sessions for muscles to recover, relax and become stronger.

Set weights used in strength training that permit you to complete at least two sets of between eight and ten repetitions per set. And you don't have to go to the gym for this stuff; you can use your own body weight, not just machines or free weights.

Learn how to stretch safely and effectively and do your stretching program every day.

The last words on the topic from Tina Palaggo-Toy are these: "the best exercises are the ones a person enjoys and will actually perform. Health benefits will be achieved regardless of what they are, and the time of the day they're done. The most important thing is to just keep moving on a daily basis."

Afterword
(Continuing Your Search for the Lost Art)

I hope you enjoyed reading *The Lost Art of General Management* and that it will help you find the general manager inside yourself and the folks you manage.

Additional readings and resources for developing your general managerial skills and talents are listed on my website, www.robwaite.com. You will find recommended books, articles, newsletters and other items that I have reviewed or have been recommended to me by trusted colleagues in my network.

If you're interested in talking to me about a speaking engagement at your company or other organization, email me at speaking@robwaite.com or give me a call at (724) 934-9625.

Rob Waite

Acknowledgements

No book is truly the work of just one person. It takes the contributions of many people, not only to complete it, but also to improve its value to readers. *The Lost Art of General Management* is no exception to this rule, and I would like to thank several people who helped make it better than it would have been, had I been left to my own devices.

I mentioned Bill Drellow, my editor, in the dedication because there wouldn't have been a book without Bill's talent and patience. Anyone looking to partner with a truly world class freelance communications professional should look into Bill's experience at www.drellow.com.

Michael Allen has been a mentor to me for ten years now. His advice was invaluable in creating this book, and I often tapped into Michael's broad and diverse business experience while I was writing it. To learn more about Michael (and to help develop your career), I highly recommend going to his CEOTRAK website (www.ceotrak.com). Michael is the founder and CEO of this impressive executive resource.

While you can't judge a book buy its cover, the cover can sure make it jump off the shelf! Faye Klein certainly caught the spirit and the intent of *The Lost Art of General Management* with her cover design. You can learn more about Faye's work at www.fayekleindesign.com.

Finally, I would like to thank James Hartigan, Commander, United States Navy, (retired). Jim's depth of leadership and strategic experience, as well as his candor, were a great help to me in writing *The Lost Art of General Management.*

Index

P

About the Author

Rob Waite is a senior executive with 20 years of leadership experience in domestic and international businesses. His successes include start-ups, turnarounds, multinational strategic partnerships and global business expansions with Fortune 500 companies and worldwide industrial leaders.

In addition to *The Lost Art of General Management*, Rob also created *The Six Figure Job Search*, an interactive CD-based seminar. Along with Zig Ziglar, Tom Hopkins, Brian Tracy and others, he has been selected to write for the *Walking With the Wise* series published by *Mentors* magazine.

Rob's career began in the college training program at Armstrong World Industries and progressed rapidly through general manager and Board member of Armstrong/HunterDouglas in the United Kingdom. Rob then joined Global 500 Lafarge SA as a vice president in its North American operations.

In early 2002, Rob was invited to join Worthington Industries' Metal Framing division as a vice president. Worthington is listed among America's Top 100 Companies to Work For by *Fortune* magazine.

Rob holds a B.A. in Business Administration from Millersville University of Pennsylvania and has completed many professional development programs, including Stanford University's *Financial Analysis and Management Program*, Penn State's *Senior Management Program*, and the Harvard Business School's *Managing the Supply Chain: The General Manager's Perspective*.

Rob lives in Wexford, Pennsylvania with his wife and three daughters.